Continuing to care
The effect on spouses and children of an older person's admission to a care home

Fay Wright

The **Joseph Rowntree Foundation** has supported this project as part of its programme of research and innovative development projects, which it hopes will be of value to policy makers and practitioners. The facts presented and views expressed in this report are, however, those of the authors and not necessarily those of the Foundation.

Published by YPS for the Joseph Rowntree Foundation

ISBN 1 899987 96 7

Cover photographs: © John Birdsall, insert © Age Concern England

Prepared and printed by:
York Publishing Services Ltd
64 Hallfield Road
Layerthorpe
York YO31 7ZQ

Contents

Acknowledgements

A study of this kind inevitably involves the support of many people. I am very grateful to the colleagues who assisted with interviews, Diane Bebbington and Alexandra Yardley. It is of great regret that Alexandra died after a short illness. My colleagues at the Age Concern Institute of Gerontology, King's College London, Professor Anthea Tinker (Professor of Social Gerontology and Director of the Institute), Professor Janet Askham (Deputy Director of the Institute), were, as usual, very supportive throughout the study. I am grateful to the care home organisations and the care home managers for facilitating the research and approaching the family caregivers. These organisations have not been named to preserve the anonymity of the respondents. The study is indebted to the daughters, sons, husbands and wives of people living in care homes for the help given to the study. I am very grateful to Liz Moore, who typed up many of the interviews, and to Emily Taylor who gracefully edited various versions of the script.

Abbreviations

ACC   Association of County Councils

ACIOG   Age Concern Institute of Gerontology

ADSS   Association of Directors of Social Services

AMA   Association of Metropolitan Authorities

CRAG   Charging for Residential Accommodation Guidance

CSO   Central Statistics Office

DH   Department of Health

DSS   Department of Social Security

GHS   General Household Survey

GP   General Practitioner

HASSASSA   Health and Social Services Adjudication and Social
           Services Adjudication Act

HMSO   Her Majesty's Stationery Office

JRF   Joseph Rowntree Foundation

LAC   Local Authority Circular

MRC   Medical Research Council

NHS   National Health Service

NISW	National Institute for Social Work
OECD	Organisation for Economic Co-operation and Development
ONS	Office of National Statistics
OPCS	Office of Population Census and Surveys
PSSRU	Personal Social Services Research Unit
SSI	Social Services Inspectorate

1 The research

Introduction

This research project funded by the Joseph Rowntree Foundation investigated the consequences for relatives of a frail older person's admission to a residential or nursing care home. In recent years considerable research attention has been given to the family caregivers of physically and mentally frail elderly people living at home. Such research has had significant implications for the expansion and development of supportive, statutory health and social services. In contrast to those numerous studies of caregiving in the community, little attention had been given in the UK to the situation of family members following a frail older person's admission to long-term residential or nursing home care.

Most UK studies use the term 'informal carer' to describe the supportive relative of a frail older person. As this seemed inappropriate and confusing for a study which includes carers employed by care homes, it was decided to use the term 'family caregiver'.

The aim of this research project was to examine significant consequences for two types of family members, spouses and middle-aged offspring, when a frail older person had been admitted to long-term residential or nursing care in the voluntary or private sector.

The research had three significant objectives, to examine:

- how family caregivers and the cared-for person chose a care home

- the costs to family members, both financial and emotional, of a cared-for person's admission to a care home

- the extent to which family caregivers continued, or wished to continue, caregiving activities in the care home.

Family caregivers in the study

A sample of 61 family caregivers including 27 spouses (11 husbands and 16 wives) and 34 adult children (24 daughters and ten sons) was selected through the managers of 35 nursing and residential care homes in the independent sector. All their relatives resident in the care homes had been admitted since 1 April 1993 when the new system of local authority funding had been introduced and all had been assessed as needing care by a local authority.

Most of the 34 adult children interviewed were middle-aged or themselves elderly. Daughters tended to be older than sons, with a mean age of 57 years. The oldest daughter was herself 72 and the youngest, 35 years old. Half the daughters were themselves aged 60 or more while the mean age of the sons was 51 years old with the oldest aged 57 years. Spouse caregivers had a mean age of 74 years and half of them were in their eighties. The oldest spouse caregiver was 90 years old and the youngest 58. Because so many daughters were in their sixties and seventies, there was no clear age differential between offspring and spouse caregivers. Many of the daughters and sons interviewed were not only themselves parents but also grandparents.

Three out of four family caregivers were owner occupiers. Sons and daughters were far more likely to be owner occupiers than spouse caregivers. Relatively few family caregivers, one in four, were in full- or part-time employment. Approximately half the daughters were in paid work, virtually all part-time, and the rest retired. Although most of the sons interviewed were economically active, several were unemployed at the time of the study.

The cared-for people

The term cared-for person is often used in this report instead of resident. Most of those being visited by family caregivers were in their eighties and nineties. Their mean age was 85 and the oldest was 101 years old. A high proportion of those being cared for, 60%, had been admitted to a care home because they were suffering from advanced dementia which made it difficult for caregivers to continue coping at home. A few people,

10%, had been admitted following a stroke. Others had diverse health problems such as advanced multiple sclerosis.

The sample

Sampling family caregivers of people resident in care homes was challenging. Although it might have been possible to find a sample through pressure groups for relatives, this would have introduced a bias because those dissatisfied with care home standards are more likely to join this type of organisation.

Initially two geographical areas were chosen and a stratified sample of independent sector care homes was drawn. Elderly Accommodation and Counsel, a voluntary organisation providing up-to-date information about alternative living options, provided detailed residential and nursing care home lists. Letters were written to managers of the sampled care homes explaining about the research and asking for assistance in identifying appropriate family caregivers. There was then a telephone follow-up to each manager who was asked to distribute explanatory letters to spouses or adult children visiting residents. After a couple of weeks these home managers were contacted by telephone again and asked for the names of any relatives agreeing to participate in the study. Although this approach resulted in a few respondents, it was not effective. Many of the private homes contacted did not have a manager regularly present on the premises. Even when managers were available communication was often problematic because they had not received the original letter. Many care homes appear to be inundated with post, much of which seems to be dropped into wastepaper bins. In any case there was little incentive for pressurised managers approached in this way to spend time and effort communicating about a research project with visiting relatives.

Four large organisations, two private and two voluntary, running residential care and nursing homes were approached and asked to support the research. When the senior managers of these organisations agreed, managers of individual homes in these organisations in four local authority areas were approached. Although this was a far more effective sampling method, it was not without problems. Some managers were interested in the research and co-operated but others pleaded pressure of work and could never find time to approach relatives. Even those managers interested in the research often reported difficulties in identifying potential respondents because they were off-duty when relatives visited. Identifying a sample of spouse caregivers was particularly difficult. Not only were there far less spouses than sons and daughters amongst family caregivers, managers were often reluctant to approach spouses because of their high level of distress. Spouses were more likely than daughters or sons both to refuse an interview initially and to back out of an interview after agreeing to take part.

Inevitably sampling through care home managers in this way introduces certain biases. Effectively managers can influence the outcomes of the research. They are likely to be reluctant to approach 'fault finding relatives' or may explain the research in such a way that relatives feel unable to participate. A small exploratory study of this kind can indicate only some of the experiences and difficulties encountered by family caregivers.

Forty-four per cent of the care homes through which the sample was drawn were in the private, for-profit sector and 56% in the voluntary, not-for-profit sector. A few of the care homes were dual registered, i.e. they had both nursing and residential care places (Table 1).

Table 1 Types of homes

Types of care homes	% of cared-for people living there
Nursing	46
Residential	44
Dual registered	10

This was a small qualitative study and can give insight only into some of the significant issues for family caregivers. As it is notoriously difficult to identify financial information in the course of a qualitative interview, financial data were collected in the first part of the interview in a very structured way with a questionnaire using showcards to assist respondents' recall. Approximately two-thirds of each interview was tape recorded and transcribed. Interviews were carried out between May and December 1996. No attempt was made to interview the care staff employed by the care homes or the cared-for person involved.

Questionnaires

Questionnaires are available from Dr Fay Wright, Age Concern Institute of Gerontology, King's College London, Cornwall House, Waterloo Road, London SE1 8WA.

The report

The following chapter sets the context for the research report. It describes:

- the demographic context

- significant changes in the provision of care homes

- the reasons why older people enter care homes

- the current debate about paying for long-term care in the future.

Chapter 3 discusses caregivers' perceptions of both the choice existing between the cared-for person remaining at home and entering a care home, and the choice available between different care homes. Financial consequences of an admission to a care home for the family caregivers involved are discussed in Chapter 4. These included both the savings made on the care costs in the community and the direct and indirect costs of the cared-for person's admission to a care home. Chapter 5 describes the role family caregivers took in a care home setting. Caregivers' views of how long-term care in homes should be paid for are discussed in Chapter 6.

2 Background issues

Introduction

Over half a million older people currently live in long-term residential or nursing home care in the UK. Some have no remaining contact with any relatives or friends living in the community, but others have offspring or even a spouse who are in contact. This study examines the consequences for daughters, sons, husbands and wives following a dependent person's admission to a residential or nursing care home. It focuses specifically on how a care home is chosen, the financial consequences for family members and the extent to which they wish, and are able, to engage in care-giving activities in a residential setting. The significance of the research findings need to be seen in the context of demographic changes in the provision of long-term institutional care and the complexities of the current system of paying for that care.

Changes in the older population

Older people today are very different in many ways from previous generations. Two features particularly relevant to this study are the changing age structures and the changes in the kinds of households in which older people live.

Increasing numbers of old people

In common with other industrialised societies the UK has experienced an unprecedented change in its population structure. Since the beginning of this century the number of people above retirement age has increased more than three-fold. The demographic trend affecting family caregivers and policy makers alike is increasing numbers of people now surviving into their eighties and nineties. Between 1961 and 1991, for example, the number of people aged 85 or over more than doubled rising from 310,000 to 812,000 (Grundy, 1995a, Table 2). Further growth in this age group is anticipated between 1991 and 2021. A projected rise of 80% would increase their numbers to 1,416,600. The significance of these increases lies in the vulnerability of people of this age. They are more likely than those who are younger to suffer greater physical or mental ill-health, and to need support from family members and from the statutory health and social services. Although only 5% of people aged 65 or over live in institutional care, those of an advanced age are more likely than those who are younger to make this move. In 1995 approximately one in four people aged 85 or over lived in a long-stay hospital or residential or nursing care home (Laing and Buisson, 1996, Table 1.2). The average age of people entering nursing or residential care has also risen. Whereas in 1989, 47% of residents in England were aged 85 or over, by 1994, the proportion at this age had increased to 54% (Central Statistical Office, 1996, p. 153).

Changes in household composition

When older people share a household with married daughters or sons, there is a greater likelihood of support in the event of illness or dependency than if they live by themselves. One of the significant changes in recent years has been in older people's living arrangements. In 1971, 27% of men and 31% of women aged 85 or over lived in complex households (i.e. with friends or relatives other than a spouse or a never-married child), but, by 1991, those proportions were only 9% and 13% respectively (Grundy, 1995a).

Changing pattern of long-term care provision

In the past 20 years the number of long-term care places has increased substantially. As Table 2 shows, in 1980 there were 89.1 places per thousand population aged 75+; by 1994 this had increased to 144.2.

The shift towards private provision

Between 1948 and about 1980, state-funded long-term care was mainly located either in NHS geriatric and mental illness hospitals or in local authority old people's homes (known as Part III). The quality of that care was, however, widely criticised (see Townsend, 1962; Willcocks *et al.*, 1987).

Table 2 Provision of long-term care places for elderly people, England, 1980–94

Year	NHS beds, general patients, elderly	Private/ voluntary nursing homes, hospitals	NHS beds, mental health, elderly	Local authority Part III residential homes	Voluntary residential homes	Private residential homes	Total all sectors	No. of places per 1,000 population aged 75+
1980	55,100			114,103	34,957	35,764	239,924	89.1
1981	54,900			114,921	36,881	39,253	245,955	89.1
1982	55,100			115,493	36,743	44,346	251,682	88.9
1983	55,600	18,200		115,913	37,613	51,760	279,086	96.0
1984	55,800	22,600		116,430	38,242	63,072	296,144	99.2
1985	55,600	27,300		116,080	37,466	80,041	316,487	103.7
1986	55,300	33,900		115,609	36,000	92,605	333,414	107.4
1987	54,600	41,600		114,189	34,374	106,108	350,871	109.9
1988	53,300	57,000	26,500	112,422	34,402	116,688	400,292	122.8
1989	51,000	73,600	25,300	109,194	34,166	135,369	428,629	128.6
1990	48,700	89,600	24,300	105,380	34,960	145,457	448,397	132.7
1991	45,900	109,000	22,500	97,853	36,685	155,315	467,253	137.1
1992	42,100	124,000	20,600	86,676	40,608	158,990	472,974	138.7
1993	40,300	144,300	19,400	77,012	43,282	162,172	486,466	144.2
1994	37,500	148,500	18,200	68,899	45,513	164,208	482,820	144.2

Source: House of Commons Health Committee, *First Report, Session 1995–96: Long-Term Care: NHS Responsibilities for Meeting Continuing Health Care Needs, Vol. 3, 1995.*

By 1980, 41% of long-term care places were in the independent sector but by 1995 this proportion had changed to 74%. Several related factors have contributed to this enormous change. As far as local authorities were concerned national monetary crises resulted in central government refusing to make further public money available for capital expenditure on Part III residential care homes. The NHS itself has undergone far-reaching changes. A sharp reduction has occurred in the number of beds for general, geriatric and older patients with mental health problems (Table 2). This decline has to be appreciated in the context of substantive increases in the throughput of patients actually being treated. Between 1979–80 and 1989–90, for example, the number of admissions almost doubled, while the average length of stay more than halved, falling from 79.3 days to 36.1 (Tinker *et al.*, 1994).

Reasons for entering residential or nursing care homes

The likelihood of an older person applying to enter a care home rises sharply with age. Women outnumber men in care homes; census figures show that older women are more than twice as likely to live in an institutional setting as their male counterparts. Not only do women tend to live longer than men, they also tend to marry men older than themselves. Most men spend their final years at home being looked after by their wives but many of their widows have no one to care for them at home and spend their final years in institutional care. Most people entering care homes have multiple disabilities and dementia is common. Although only between 1% and 7% of people over the age of 65 suffer from some form of dementia, its prevalence increases markedly with age and as many as 20% of those aged 80 or more may be affected (Askham and Thompson, 1990).

A review of research carried out for the Wagner Committee on residential care issues concluded that the difficulties of maintaining a person in the community are greater if dependency stems from dementia rather than from physical incapacity (Sinclair, 1988). Behavioural problems associated with dementia are particularly stressful. Several studies have demonstrated the impact of these problems on carers' stress levels (Levin *et al.*, 1989, 1994; Askham and Thompson, 1990). One of these studies that re-interviewed carers of dementia sufferers after an interval of a year concluded that the only two factors resulting in a reduction of a carer's stress levels were a dementia sufferer's death or permanent admission to long-term care (Levin *et al.*, 1994).

A Social Services Inspectorate (SSI) study in seven authorities focused on the F (fear) factor underlying many admissions to residential care, i.e. fear of falls, general anxiety and insecurity, fear of attack and fear of being unable to cope (SSI/DH, 1994). Other studies of newly-admitted residents draw similar conclusions about the reasons for admission (Neill *et al.*, 1988; Allen *et al.*, 1992; Phillips, 1992). All these studies also draw the conclusion that the initiative to enter long-term care was far more likely to lie with a relative, or a professional such as a GP, than with the resident concerned. For example, only 22% of a sample of frail older people recently admitted to residential or nursing home care in three local authorities reported that they themselves had taken the initiative (Allen *et al.*, 1992). Relatives had been the most likely source of pressure over admission to a home. Another study of 200 predominantly middle-class residents in 39 private homes in Suffolk drew similar conclusions about the initiative to enter long-term care (Philips, 1992). Both studies, carried out before the implementation of the NHS and Community Care Act in 1993, concluded that most newly-admitted residents felt that a choice between staying at home and entering a home had been non-existent because of the inadequacy of support services in the community.

Bereavement or a lack of relatives who can give support in the community makes an application for admission to long-term care more likely (Willcocks *et al.*, 1987; Sinclair, 1988), but by no means all of those entering care are widowed or single. Although there are no official up-to-date figures for the total number of elderly married people in long-term residential or nursing home care, the 1991 Census gives some information. Altogether just under 50,000 married older men and women were resident in communal establishments in Great Britain; 52% of them were women and 48% men (Office of Population, Census and Surveys, 1993, Table 3). In effect, this means that approximately one in ten people in long-term care are married. Some married residents would have a spouse also in a care home but most would have a spouse living in the community. On the whole, however, married men and women aged 65 or over are far less likely to live in institutional care than those who are not married.

Sources of finance for long-term care

Four main sources of funding for long-term care exist:

- public funding
- personal income or capital
- charitable funding
- financial support from relatives.

Payment is often from a combination of these sources.

Public funding
The four main sources of public funding are:

• the National Health Service (NHS)

• the old 'preserved' system of income support for people in long-term care before 31 March 1993

• the new system of local authority funding

• ordinary social security benefits.

The National Health Service
The NHS accepts financial responsibility for a small proportion of long-stay places in independent sector nursing homes. Current estimates are that 7% of places are paid for in this way (Laing and Buisson, 1996, Table 7.7). Fees paid under NHS contracts are substantially higher than those paid by local authorities, reflecting the higher level of dependency for which the NHS accepts financial responsibility (Laing and Buisson, 1996, p. 114). As the NHS is not allowed to charge patients, people in NHS-funded places are not expected to pay from savings for their care. Inevitably, as most people resident in care homes have to meet some or all of their costs, this arrangement giving a minority free NHS care has been widely criticised as unfair. A hospital stay has some financial penalties, however, as certain social security benefits are either reduced or stopped after a few weeks.

Central government has issued guidance in this area. A circular to health and local authorities, HSG (95) 8 LAC (95) 5, sought to limit the financial responsibility of the NHS by promoting a clearer definition of elderly people's rights to free NHS continuing care. Eligibility criteria are locally defined: health authorities have to produce local policies in consultation with independent home providers as well as representatives of users and carers.

If patients and their families disagree with the health authority's decision on eligibility they have a right to refer the decision to an independent panel. A recent House of Commons Health Committee report (1995/96a, par. 68) strongly recommended that a national framework be developed to include national eligibility criteria 'to define what the NHS as a service will provide'.

The old 'preserved' system of income support

People living permanently in independent sector care homes before 31 March 1993 have a 'preserved right' to the income support system in operation at that time. Not only do residents who were already claimants continue to receive preserved system income support rates, those paying privately before that date are entitled to claim under the same system if savings drop to £16,000. They will, however, have to pay part of their fees until capital is reduced to £10,000.

This old preserved system of income support set national flat rate benefit limits. Some variation in the limits exists between nursing and residential homes, and between different degrees of disability. Although higher rates are paid for care homes in Greater London, there are no other geographical variations.

Research funded by the Joseph Rowntree Foundation shows that 52% of those with preserved rights pay higher fees than the preserved rights income support limits (Laing, 1998). Although in half these cases the difference is less than the personal expenses allowance and would usually be met by the resident, in the remainder the difference is greater. In these circumstances relatives and charities get involved in topping up the income support.

Inevitably the proportion of residents with preserved rights to the old income support system has been in decline. At May 1995, 37% of elderly and physically handicapped residents in nursing and residential homes were wholly or partly financed by the preserved income support system (Laing and Buisson, 1996, Table 7.9).

New system of local authority funded long-term care
A new funding system was introduced by the 1990 NHS and
Community Care Act. From April 1993 local authorities became the
principal budget holders for state funding. With the exception of the
small number of people placed directly in nursing homes by health
authorities, local authorities now assess people wanting to enter
residential or nursing home care. This assessment is both of a need for
such care and of an individual's financial means. A person entering an
independent sector care home and assessed as needing this level of care
by a local authority is entitled to income support at the same rate as a
person of the same age living at home in the community plus an
additional flat rate residential allowance.

Although central government has issued manager and practitioner
guides for care management and assessment, local authorities have been
able to develop their own criteria and systems. Each local authority now
has its own system for assessment and provision of services. According
to a recent Audit Commission report (1996), eligibility criteria for
admission to residential or nursing home care varies widely and many
authorities, particularly those under financial pressure, find the whole
process of setting criteria difficult. In assessing how much a resident
should pay towards the cost of care, however, a local authority has to
follow national rules which are similar, but not identical, to income
support rules.

Despite the 1990 Act heralding innovative processes for allocating state
funding, there was no change in the fundamental underlying principle
that the individual concerned has prime responsibility to pay for care. In
assessing how much a resident should pay towards her or his care, a
local authority has to take into account all income and capital. Income
would include social security benefits such as retirement pensions or
income support and any occupational or personal pensions. With the
exception of an amount specified by central government to cover
personal expenses (currently at 1 April 1998, £14.45) a local authority
will recoup any social security benefits from a resident. In effect this
system is an elaborate way of transferring money from central to local
government. Not surprisingly many relatives handling financial

transfers on behalf of a resident either by collecting payments from a post office or arranging direct bank payments are bemused at their role in this transfer process.

Capital has to include savings of all kinds and the value of a house if a resident previously lived alone and was an owner occupier. If a house has not been sold before the individual concerned entered a care home a local authority is empowered to place a charge against it and to recover care costs *with interest* when the property is finally sold (Laing, 1993). A local authority cannot enforce the sale of a property without first obtaining a court order. A court would consider what would be fair in the individual circumstances of each case and can take into consideration the presence of someone in the home, the size of outstanding debt compared to the value of the asset and the effect on other creditors (National Consumer Council, 1995, Appendix E). A house has to be counted as part of a person's capital unless lived in by a partner or a spouse, a relative over the age of 60 or a relative under the age of 60 who is incapacitated, or a child under 16 who the resident is liable to maintain. In these circumstances a local authority has to ignore the value of the property.

Capital disregard. For many years no account was taken of capital up to £3,000. Capital between £3,000 and £8,000 was regarded as producing a notional income (£1 for each £250, or part of, held). Capital over £8,000 was assumed to be wholly available to pay for residential care. On 8 April 1996 the limits were increased substantially: the bottom limit was increased from £3,000 to £10,000 and the top from £8,000 to £16,000.

Deliberate deprivation. Strategies to circumvent the assessment rules and to prevent capital and income being used to meet the costs of care may be adopted prior to an individual applying for admission to a care home. These might include an older person transferring a house to their children or placing savings in their children's bank accounts. If assets have been given away within six months of a person entering a care home, a local authority can recover from the recipient(s) the money owed in respect of a place (section 21 of the Health and Social Services and Social Security Adjudication Act 1983, HASSASSA). But, if the transfer of moneys or property took place more than six months before an individual's entry to a home, a local authority cannot reclaim the money directly from a third party. If it is felt that the transfer was made to avoid paying fees, the local authority can charge a resident taking into account 'notional' income or capital (this section of HASSASSA was implemented in 1993). DSS guidance on deprivation of assets requires local authorities to bear in mind that individuals may dispose of assets without deliberately aiming for deprivation. The CRAG (Charging for Residential Accommodation Guide) rules require the following points to be borne in mind:

> *There may be more than one purpose in disposing of an account, only one of which is to avoid a charge for accommodation. Avoiding the charge need not be a resident's main motive but must be a significant one ... The timing of the disposal should be taken into account when considering the purpose of the disposal. It would be unreasonable to decide that a resident had disposed of an asset in order to reduce his charge for accommodation when the disposal took place at a time when he was fit and healthy and could not have foreseen the need for a move to residential accommodation.* (Department of Social Security, 1995a, par. 6.062–6.064)

Geographical differences in what residents may have to pay. Residents who have capital above the limits and have been assessed by a local authority will have to meet the negotiated care home fee in full. Geographical variations do exist between local authorities in the fee levels negotiated with independent sector providers. Individual local authorities decide on local fees that they will pay for different types of care in independent sector homes. Such baselines are generally arrived at in consultation with local home owners' associations (Association of County Councils, 1993). According to an Association of County Councils (ACC) survey, most authorities make a 'take it or leave it' offer to care home managers on baseline fees for different categories of care (Edwards and Kenny, 1995). The third national survey of fees and fee negotiations reported that, with the exception of London and the Thames and Anglia regions, average costs were close to DSS rates (Kenny, 1997). Local authorities in London and the Home Counties have consistently paid considerably higher baseline fees than those paid by local authorities in other parts of the country. In 1994, for example, only one authority in London had an upper ceiling for residential and nursing care at the income support level for those with preserved rights (Kenny and Edwards, 1995). Both the scarcity and the high cost of nursing and residential care places in London boroughs is reflected in a high proportion of placements outside their boundaries.

Ordinary social security benefits

There are circumstances in which an older person (and an involved relative) may prefer to use social security benefits to pay care home fees rather than have local authority involvement. An attendance or disabled living allowance may be paid to a person with a defined level of disability living at home and continue to be payable if that person becomes a private payer in an independent sector care home. Such allowances would cease four weeks after an admission if a local authority took financial responsibility. Income support, a residential allowance and various other income support premiums may also be payable. These combined social security benefits would bring people close to being able to pay care home fees at the lower end of the market even if there are no savings to use (Wistow and Henwood, 1994; Laing and Buisson, 1996). Different rules in respect of the treatment of capital also encourage this course of action. Since April 1996, a person in a care home is eligible for income support when savings fall below £16,000 but, in contrast, an older person living in the community would be eligible for income support only if savings were under £8,000.

Because central and local governments have different rules in respect of property, there may be considerable financial advantages to entering a care home without a local authority assessment if a resident has a house to sell and savings under £16,000. In this situation a person would be eligible for income support and a flat rate residential allowance. Until a house is sold these social security benefits would be payable for up to six months (or longer in certain circumstances). Completion of a house sale would usually lead to benefits being withdrawn. This arrangement has an advantage for the consumer because the Department of Social Security does not demand repayment of benefits (Age Concern England, 1996a). When a local authority accepts financial responsibility the situation is different. A legal charge could be put against a property and at the completion of the sale the full cost of care would be recouped from the proceeds.

A review of this route into residential care concluded that both independent sector home providers and local authorities gained from encouraging its use (Henwood and Wistow, 1995). For their part home providers would avoid dependency on local authority contracts if people entered care homes without a local authority assessment. Local authorities themselves would save money if people used central government sources of money. A large number of people are thought to be using this loophole. In 1994 an estimated 98,500 recipients of the attendance or the disabled living allowance were living in independent sector homes (Joseph Rowntree Foundation Inquiry, 1996, p. 18). Using this loophole route carries considerable risks, however, for the older person concerned. An Age Concern factsheet pointed out that the government could close this loophole at any time (Age Concern, 1996a). Although combined social security benefits might be sufficient to pay a care home's fee initially, there is no guarantee that fees would stay at a particular level and fees could be raised. In addition a person's care needs may change and it may become necessary to pay for a higher level of care in the same home or to move to a different and more expensive home.

Personal income or capital
Although state funding is so important in paying for long-term care, a significant proportion of residents, 28%, are self-payers in the sense that they use their own income and capital to meet fees in addition to the social security benefits to which they may be entitled (Table 3). Virtually all of these residents, for example, would be entitled to state retirement pensions.

A relatively low proportion of elderly people could afford to pay for their own long-term care just from normal income. It has been suggested that only about 10% of those aged 70 or over would be in this position, assuming the need for disposable income at least twice the relevant income support levels (Oldman, 1991).

Capital
By far the most important source of capital for people going into long-term care is property. Home ownership is the single most important source of wealth for about half the population. Growth of owner

Table 3 Source of finance for residents in private and voluntary nursing and residential homes for elderly and physically handicapped people, Great Britain, February 1994

Funding source	Nursing homes		Residential homes		Total	
	000s	%	000s	%	000s	%
Income support	67	38	69	36	137	37
Local authorities	51	29	40	20	120	32
NHS	13	7	-	-	13	13
Self-pay	47	27	62	32	103	28
Total	169	100	194	100	372	100

Sources: Laing and Buisson, 1996, Table 7.7, derived from *Income Support Statistics Quarterly Enquiry February 25 1994: Residential Care and Nursing Home Report.* Department of Social Security.

occupation has been one of the most significant trends since the Second World War. In 1981, 54% of people in all socio-economic groups were owner occupiers and by 1995/96 the proportion had risen to 68% (Office of National Statistics, 1997, Table 10.2). Owner occupation is not spread evenly, however, through all age groups. Elderly people are less likely to be owner occupiers than the middle-aged. General Household Survey figures show that, whereas 79% of those in the 45–59 age group currently own their own houses, this is the case for only 55% of those aged 80 or over (Office of National Statistics, 1997, Table 10.34). Nevertheless these figures do indicate that the proportion of older people who are owner occupiers will certainly increase as people who are currently middle-aged get older. A significant aspect of this phenomenon is regional variation in house ownership. As a study of housing wealth in later life points out, at one extreme, 68.8% of older households in Wales own their own home compared with 36.6% of older households in Scotland (Gibbs and Oldman, 1993).

The significance of housing as such a source of wealth lies in the substantial increase in house prices which has taken place. According to the Building Societies Association there were three major periods of house price inflation in the 1970s and 1980s when the national average house price rose from £5,000 in 1969 to £60,000 in 1989 (Hamnett, 1995a).

Funding by voluntary organisations

Many voluntary organisations are extensively involved in financing elderly people in long-term care. Two significant ways in which this occurs are: voluntary organisations running a care home at a loss because a local authority baseline fee is lower than care home charges and topping up income support.

Financial support from relatives

Different categories of family members have different legal financial responsibilities. Daughters or sons are not considered to be liable relatives and cannot be asked as a matter of course to contribute to the cost of a parent's care. If a care home is preferred that has fees higher than the local authority baseline, they may choose to top up the amount a local authority is prepared to pay. This is more likely to happen for residents admitted before April 1993 than after.

A spouse's financial liability

Spouses are in a very different situation from offspring. Under Section 42 of the 1948 National Assistance Act a man is liable to maintain his wife and a woman her husband. This means that if one married partner is admitted to residential or nursing home care a local authority can ask the spouse remaining in the community to contribute towards the costs. An unmarried partner, on the other hand, has no legal obligation to pay for a partner's care. A local authority asking a husband or wife to contribute, however, does not have the power to means-test the spouse remaining at home and declaration of income and assets are voluntary. If no voluntary agreement can be reached, a local authority may make a complaint to a magistrate's court which would have the power to decide how much a liable relative should pay (West, 1995). Although no research evidence exists about how local authorities interpret their powers, there are grounds for thinking that interpretations will vary. Considerable evidence exists, for example, of misunderstandings within local authorities of the legal position in respect to community support services. Although only the resources of the person getting a service in the community should be taken into account, carers and other members of the household have often been asked to pay charges (Bronsbury, 1995).

Spouses and pensions

As far as the state retirement pension for a married couple is concerned the spouse remaining at home is entitled to half and the partner in a care home to half. The value of this half pension is taken fully into account in estimating how much a married resident should contribute towards the costs of care. A spouse remaining in the community is left with a pension equivalent to half a couple's state retirement pension which is worth considerably less than a full single person's pension.

Occupational pension schemes have become an important source of income, particularly for younger pensioners. Recent figures for 1993 show that 54% of recently retired single pensioners and 75% of couples had an occupational pension (Department of Social Security, 1996a, Table B2.05). Over a third (34%) of the recently retired, therefore, received no occupational pension at all. Even when there is an occupational pension, its value may not be very great. The average occupational pension for these recently retired pensioners was £55.70 per week for a single pensioner and £104.20 for a couple (Department of Social Security, 1996a). Women are less likely then men to pay into an occupational pension scheme. A recent General Household Survey showed that in 1993–94, 60% of men and 54% of women in full-time work were paying into such a scheme (Central Statistical Office, 1996, Table 5.22). Contributing to an occupational pension scheme varies with socio-economic group. Middle-class people are more likely to pay into a scheme than those in other types of occupations. In 1993–94, for example, around three-quarters of professional and intermediate non-manual workers were members of their employer's pension scheme compared with only two-fifths of semi-skilled and manual workers (Central Statistical Office, 1996, p. 112).

Prior to 1996 a resident's occupational pension was taken fully into account in assessing how much had to be paid towards a care home's charges. As husbands are more likely than wives to have an occupational pension, this ruling was more likely to be operational when a married man was admitted to a care home. In effect this often meant considerable hardship for a wife left living in the community, because the whole occupational pension was taken. Since April 1996 local authorities must ignore half of any occupational pension paid to a married resident provided that at least half the pension is being paid to the spouse remaining in the community (Secretary of State for Health, 1996, par. B.9). A resident's occupational pension can be counted as a couple's joint income and split into two equal parts.

Approved personal pension plans were introduced in 1988. Such schemes have been encouraged by the government and are intended to offer pensions to those who do not have access to an occupational pension scheme. Private pensions have proved highly popular and by 1993 almost six million people including two million women had taken them up (Williams and Field, 1993). Recent General Household Survey figures show that 29% of men in full-time employment and 22% of women are paying into personal pension plans (Central Statistical Office, 1996, Table 5.22). A personal pension like an occupational pension can be split into two parts.

Spouses and savings
Although a couple with joint savings are entitled to divide them into two unequal parts to avoid the spouse in a care home from being assessed as having half the couple's total savings, it is uncertain how often this right is realised and put into practice.

Spouses and the personal expenses allowance
In special circumstances, the amount of the personal expenses allowance paid to a resident receiving income support may be varied. Local authorities have the discretion to increase the allowance in order that additional income can be passed to the spouse remaining at home. It is thought that this power is rarely invoked.

Current debate about paying for long-term care in the future

There is currently widespread debate in the UK about how long-term care for older people who are frail or disabled should be paid for in the future. This debate is being echoed in many other industrialised societies (OECD, 1996). It is being stimulated by common concerns about the substantial growth in the numbers of older people aged 80 and over, the future availability of support from family members and mounting public costs. Although the inequities of the current system have been widely acknowledged there is no consensus on the right potential policy options for paying for long-term care in the future.

A House of Commons Health Committee (1995/96a,b) has taken evidence and made recommendations on future provision and funding. The previous government produced a consultation paper *A New Partnership for Care in Old Age*, setting out the options and recommending the development of a partnership scheme based on indemnity insurance (Secretary of State for Health, 1996). The Joseph Rowntree Foundation Inquiry (1996) recommended a number of changes including separating care costs and accommodation costs for long-term care and introducing a new compulsory insurance scheme. At the time of writing, a Royal Commission on Long-Term Care for the Elderly is gathering evidence and will make recommendations in December 1998.

3 Choice

Introduction

This chapter focuses on why family caregivers and those being cared for choose a care home and how the choice was made between different care homes. During the past 20 years there has been growing concern about the extent of choices open to frail older people and to family caregivers. The idea of a choice implies a right or power to make a choice and, then, having a variety from which to choose. A caregiver's right to choice may well conflict with a dependent person's rights. If the caregiver does not wish, or is unable, to continue providing support to a frail person in the community, the frail person concerned may nevertheless want that support to continue. As this study focused on family caregivers' perspectives, the voice of the person being cared for is absent. This chapter, then, focuses on issues of choice primarily for the caregivers.

It therefore begins by considering current good practice guidance relating to choice and to entry into care homes. The choices perceived by the caregivers in relation to the cared-for person remaining at home or entering institutional care are then discussed. Family caregivers' involvement in choosing a care home and the factors appearing to influence choice are discussed in the final section.

Good practice guidance on choice

The importance of choice has been discussed in various official good practice guidance. In respect of care homes these include an independent review of residential care chaired by Lady Wagner, *A Positive Choice* (Wagner, 1988) and two Social Services Inspectorate (SSI) handbooks on how to evaluate quality of care and quality of life in residential care homes for elderly people, *Homes are for Living in* and *Caring for Quality: Guidance on Standards for Residential Homes for Elderly People* (Department of Health\SSI, 1989, 1990). Two codes of practice resulting from working parties convened by the Centre for Policy on Ageing (CPA), *Home Life* and *A Better Home Life* (CPA, 1984, 1996) are used widely. The earlier CPA publication focused on residential care only and the latter on both residential and nursing home care. A booklet to assist frail older people and caregivers understand more about the processes and procedures for entering a care home, *Moving into a Care Home: Things You Need to Know*, has also been issued by the Department of Health (1996). As so many older people enter care homes following hospitalisation, two SSI reports on social services department arrangements for discharge of older people from hospital to care homes, *Moving On* and *Moving On: A Further Year*, contain relevant guidance (Department of Health\SSI, 1995a,b).

Several themes relating to choice and entry into care homes appear in these good practice guides.

1   *A real choice should exist between remaining at home with an adequate and appropriate package of support services and entering residential or nursing home care.* No one should be obliged to change their permanent accommodation in order to receive services which could be made available to them in their own homes (Wagner, 1988, p. 114).

2   *Even when older people are confused or demented they should be involved as far as possible in the decision to enter residential or nursing home care.* Having choice and being involved in negotiation, even where choice is restricted, can be a positive and rewarding experience for everyone involved (Wagner, 1988, p. 9).

3   *A choice should exist between different homes.* Furthermore, a 'good' home will have been selected from a range of options as an informed choice by the resident, with involvement of relatives and other advisers as appropriate to his or her ability to exercise choice (Department of Health\SSI, 1989, p. 82).

4   *Written information in the form of a brochure (required under the 1984 Registered Homes Act) should be available to residents and their relatives to assist them in making choices.* All homes should make available a brochure prospectus which sets out the aims and objectives of the

management including the type of resident catered for, the degree of care offered, the extent to which illness or disability can be accommodated and any restrictions relating to age, sex, religion, etc. The brochure should also accurately describe the facilities, staffing and accommodation offered and may include terms and conditions (Centre for Policy on Ageing, 1984, p. 18 par. 2.1.1).

The DH leaflet issued to clarify the process and procedures for entering care homes sets out how a social services department can help a person make the right choice. A department should be considering:

- giving you the information about homes – you do not have to choose one from the list they suggest

- helping you visit any home you are considering

- arranging a short trial stay in a home before you finally choose

- showing you the latest local authority inspection report on how the home is run (Department of Health, 1996, p. 14).

The 1990 NHS and Community Care Act itself contains a Direction on Choice. Local authorities are required by the Secretary of State to arrange a place in a care home of a person's choice providing certain conditions are met. These are that:

- a place is available, and the home is willing to arrange a contract according to the local authority's terms and conditions

- the place is suitable for the person's assessed needs

- the place does not cost more than the authority would 'usually' expect to pay for someone with the same assessed needs (Meredith, 1995b, p. 101).

However local authorities' interpretations of this Direction vary by area (Meredith, 1995b). Recent government guidance makes it clear that people can consider moving into a care home that costs more than a social services department is prepared to pay 'if someone else like a relative, friend or charity is prepared to pay the balance for as long as you are in the home' (Department of Health, 1996, p. 16).

A choice between remaining at home and entering a care home?

A key factor in a frail older person continuing to live at home is the amount of support needed. Family caregivers in the sample were asked whether the cared-for person had needed help with personal care (such as bathing, dressing, using the toilet, or eating a meal) or with ordinary household tasks (such as cleaning, cooking or shopping) in the period before admission to a care home. If help had been needed information was obtained about who provided it and whether it had to be paid for (for a discussion of the costs of care in the community see the following chapter). As in other studies of caregiving by adult children and spouses, on both sides of the Atlantic, there was no doubt that people supported by a spouse before finally being admitted to a care home were likely to be more dependent in respect of personal care and doing any housework than those supported by a daughter or son (Wenger, 1984; Townsend, 1990). The only area of personal care where this was not the case was in taking a bath. Few people supported by either a spouse or an adult child were able to take a bath without assistance. When help was needed with any aspect of personal care or with any household task, spouses were far more likely than adult children to give personal assistance. Co-residence is a key factor in the greater caregiving burden of spouses. As Arber and Ginn (1991) pointed out from a re-analysis of the 1985 General Household Survey the average amount of time spent by co-resident carers is almost six times greater than the amount of time spent by those caring for an older person in another household. Although spouses in the present study were co-resident this was the case for only two of the daughters and none of the sons.

Support from the statutory services

Good practice guidance, as already outlined, is that an appropriate and adequate package of care should be available to frail older people living in their own homes. A wide range of different types of support for many of the cared-for people from either social services or the community health services was described. These included home care assistants coming into the home to assist with personal care such as bathing or dressing, meals-on-wheels, cleaning and day care. In addition a few caregivers reported support being purchased directly from private agencies. Some differences between family caregivers were in evidence. Daughters and sons were twice as likely as spouses to report that there had been a package of two or more types of support from the statutory services coming into the home. Spouses as a whole, on the other hand, were more likely than sons or daughters to report that the cared-for person had attended a day centre on at least one day of the week. Almost half the cared-for people were reported to have been attending a day centre in the period before admission to institutional care. Wife caregivers were the group least likely to have support from the statutory services with any personal care task. They were also less likely than husbands to have had the cared-for person attend a day centre.

Other studies confirm that day care is rarely used extensively. A study of residential homes with day centres attached, for example, reported that virtually all day centre users attended only for one or two days of the week (Wright, 1995). Although day care is rarely extensive, it is very significant, particularly for co-resident caregivers in giving respite from the caring burden. Even when caregivers are not co-resident, a parent attending a day centre can give reassurance that at least the day is being passed in a sociable situation with a meal provided and care staff on call.

Although wife caregivers were the least likely to receive support, they appeared to be the most likely to have turned down any support offered. For example, one of the wives, who had found it increasingly difficult to cope with a husband who had Parkinson's disease and had become too confused to look after himself in any way, admitted that she had rejected offers of help:

> *They kept saying, 'Would you like any help?' But what's the point? I mean he was going* [to the toilet] *three or four times a day. I couldn't call anybody in to help with that. And then they said, 'Do you want anybody to undress him and put him to bed?' They would only have come here at times like 6.30 p.m. So I just said, 'No'.*

Indeed a common complaint about home care staff was arriving at inappropriate times. If the cared-for person was assisted in getting to bed too early or too late in the evening, the arrangement could cause considerable distress:

> *When she had these home aiders there, they used to give her tea and get her ready for bed about 6 o'clock. Well I think she used to go off to sleep in the chair, wake up, think it was morning and get dressed; because it was so early to get her ready for bed.* (Daughter)

> *For a short time the local authority did provide helpers to come here to get her up in the morning and to put her to bed at night. This wasn't terribly satisfactory because getting her up they would come any time up to midday, sometimes even as late as that, and at night-time, sometimes at midnight, which really wasn't at all good.* (Husband)

A changeover of responsibility between the community health services and social services could threaten care continuing in the community. One of the wives became very distressed as the level of care for her bedridden husband plummeted:

> *The district nursing system was handing over a lot of the care to social services; something to do with funding. This is where things became difficult because Jim had a colostomy and untrained nurses can't really deal with colostomies. But they were expected to. I couldn't understand this. He was having catheter problems too.*

This decline in the standard of care in the home led to the wife looking for a place in a nursing home to obtain better quality nursing care.

Some of those being cared for at home could be only too ready themselves to cancel services. Several parents were reported to have cancelled meals-on-wheels.

> *They did start her on meals-on-wheels but then she got so she was buying them and then just parcelling them up – for the dog, which was a total waste of time. So after a few weeks I stopped that.* (Daughter)

*I went round one night and she said, 'I haven't had any dinner today'. So
I said, 'Why not, why didn't you tell me they had not been?' So she said, 'I
told them yesterday I can't be doing with all these meals coming in at odd
times during the day. I told them not to bother.'* (Daughter)

Some daughters and sons interviewed felt that a parent had had to enter
a care home because the social and health services would not or could
not provide enough support. Several daughters and sons expressed the
view that:

She could have remained at home if there had been 24-hour cover.

This question of providing extensive support in the home is important
because of the high cost involved. As the Audit Commission (1996)
pointed out, the financial incentive for local authorities to use residential
care remains strong because it is substantially cheaper to place people in
residential care even when there is no difference between the cost of a
residential place and care at home. This 'perverse incentive' arises from
local authorities being unable to take the value of a person's home into
account when charging for a package of support in an individual's own
home. Conversely if a placement is made in a residential care or nursing
home there is a nationally determined means test and a local authority
takes income and assets, including any property, into account.

Family caregivers may also have a perverse incentive to arrange a
placement in a care home. Although daughters and sons cannot
currently be charged for a care package in the community this is not the
case for a spouse. One of the wives interviewed had agreed to her
husband entering a care home only because she was unable to afford
local authority charges for an extensive package of care at home. Her
husband had suffered a stroke and was unable to care for himself in any
way and she herself lacked the physical strength to cope with the lifting
involved:

*I was told that I could have him at home and I could have someone to come
in and dress him in the morning for an hour and someone to come in at
lunchtime to see to his toilet needs for three-quarters of an hour and*

someone at night to help undress him and get him into bed. And that would cost me £200 a week. I could not afford it.

An end to caregiving at home

Few family caregivers thought that the caring situation could have continued much longer at home. Inevitably virtually all the admissions to a care home had been precipitated by a crisis. Sometimes the crisis occurred at home and there was a direct admission to a care home. In most cases, however, the cared-for person was admitted to hospital following a crisis such as a stroke, a fall or a fracture and entry to a care home followed hospital discharge. With the exception of those who had suffered strokes, a cared-for person's life before admission had generally been a period of increasing dependency.

A crisis at home

The stresses and strains for family caregivers supporting frail older people living in the community have by now been well documented in an extensive literature (Finch and Groves, 1983; Twigg and Atkin, 1994). Co-resident caregiving can be particularly traumatic as a caregiver is likely to find difficulties in leading any kind of independent life. When a cared-for person has dementia the problems are often extreme (Askham and Thompson, 1990; Levin *et al.*, 1989, 1994). The types of crises in the current study contributing to caring situations coming to an end included:

- a caregiver's own health problems

- sleep deprivation

- inability to cope with incontinence

- inability to cope physically with care tasks.

When the cared-for person suffered from dementia a combination of crises on several fronts often precipitated an admission to a care home.

A caregiver's own health problems could make it difficult to continue providing care at home. Several daughters, whose mothers needed physical help in getting into a bath or with getting out of bed or with dressing, reported being unable to continue because of serious back problems:

> *I do have a bad back, I've had that problem going back about 20 years. I was in hospital. Last year, no the year before last now, I was away six months with back problems, and I've also had a breast off as well. So that's one of the reasons I couldn't possibly look after Mum; because if she was to fall I wouldn't be able to pick her up or do anything, if she needed help I wouldn't be able to do it.* (Daughter)

The spouses interviewed were more likely than the daughters and sons to report serious health problems. High blood pressure and angina were mentioned by several. One of the husbands, for example, felt unable to continue looking after his wife following heart bypass surgery.

Not surprisingly sleep deprivation had become exhausting to some co-resident caregivers. In all cases those being cared for were Alzheimer's disease sufferers who failed to distinguish between day and night. One of the husbands described his wife's high level of activity during the night which made it impossible for him to sleep. It became difficult for him to concentrate on his job the next day:

> *And then we had a period of when she talked constantly all night, as though she was on the phone. The sentences she came out with were understandable, but it was just as though she was talking to somebody on the phone. And this would go on all night, it would go on sometimes for three nights consecutively. And then she'd go to the day hospital to sleep all day, and I had to work!*

Sleep deprivation drove one of the husbands to abandon caring after several years:

> *I got to the point when I was at the end of my tether. I'd had no sleep for four or five nights. For the nth time I'd had no sleep for ages. I took her up to the Emergency Department at the hospital and dumped her ... I said, 'I just can't look after her now. You're going to have to take her'.*

Incontinence has been identified as a particularly stressful aspect of caring (Levin *et al.*, 1989) and is likely to be embarrassing to both caregiver and the person being cared for. It poses practical problems such as laundering bedding and clothing. If the dependent person suffers from dementia and is unable or unwilling to co-operate in protecting bedding and clothing, the situation can become extremely difficult. Some husbands described the cared-for person's incontinence as the main reason for seeking institutional care:

No, I threw in the towel, putting it mildly, when she became incontinent. I thought, 'No I can't cope with this'. I'd coped so far.

She was at home as much as possible. But when it got to the state as I said with the incontinence that was the biggest trouble really.

Some of the wives experienced problems with a dependent spouse being doubly incontinent, but never gave it as a reason for caregiving at home coming to an end. A study of caring across a variety of relationships concluded that cross-gender caring appears to be more problematic when provided by males for females (Twigg and Atkin, 1994, p. 32). Although it is often assumed that spouses can and should support each other, a situation in which one spouse is dependent has its own difficulties. As Parker (1993) pointed out in a study of husbands and wives below retirement age caring for a disabled spouse, providing intimate personal care is not made easier by marriage. It may be made more difficult because it can constrain a couple's sexual relationship in both subtle, and not so subtle, ways.

No less than 40% of the spouse caregivers interviewed were aged 75 or over. A significant problem described by some of them was that they themselves no longer had sufficient strength to cope with the heavy physical work involved in tending a partner with severe disabilities. Not surprisingly lifting was cited as particularly difficult:

No, I don't think so. As I say, she can't stand or walk – she has to be lifted about. I mean she just can't do it. I couldn't manage; they'd have to pick me off the floor. I couldn't manage. (Husband)

Although gadgets could relieve some of the physical strain, they often did not eliminate it entirely. A wife caring for a husband who had very limited movement because of advanced multiple sclerosis described the effort needed to use a hoist:

I started to have pains in my wrists and pains in my chest. I had to go to casualty with chest pains – my daughter insisted – she thought it was heart trouble but all it was was strain and stress. My wrists started hurting a lot. We have an electric hoist. That only pulls him up and down and across. It doesn't actually turn his body. There's still a lot of work involved. (Wife)

If a caregiver is old and frail as so many spouses were, then a caring situation can only too easily be terminated by an accident. A husband himself in poor health seemed relieved that his own accident had put an end to continuing to provide care at home:

I was going to visit my wife in hospital by bus and I stopped beside the building for a rest. After about three or four minutes I started off again. All of a sudden I went down hard on the right knee – on the lame leg as it were. I couldn't get up so they got a wheelchair and took me to casualty and discovered I'd fractured it … I think that made them change their mind about my wife being at home. (Husband)

Family caregivers in the present study were asked if they thought that any extra types of support or services might have made any difference to the cared-for person remaining at home. Few thought that anything could have really made any difference. They were, of course, being interviewed after the decision had been taken that a care home was necessary. Spouses in particular described themselves as overwhelmed by problems such as sleep deprivation or difficult behaviour or being unable to cope physically with lifting – problems that are difficult for community support services to address. Although offspring were more likely to report care packages for the cared-for person, they were also likely to feel either that the amount of support was inadequate or that it was available at inappropriate times. They had no confidence that such a situation would have improved.

Hospitalisation
A high proportion of the cared-for people, two out of three, had been
admitted to a care home directly from hospital. Various crises such as
falls, fractures or strokes had led to the hospital admission. With the
exception of the people who had suffered strokes, the cared-for person's
life before hospitalisation had been one of increasing dependency. An
accident or illness not only threatens a cared-for person's ability to
remain at home, it also allows a family caregiver a chance to re-assess the
feasibility of continuing to give support.

Over half the caregivers of people admitted to care homes following
hospital discharge reported feeling under pressure to move the cared-for
person out of hospital. Two sources of pressure were reported: hospital
staff wanting beds emptied and poor quality of care in the hospital. For
their part, hospital staff themselves may be under considerable pressure.
An overall decline in hospital beds, an accelerated throughput of
patients and a marked reduction in the number of nursing staff
employed must mean that the pressure to release beds becomes intense.
As the Social Services Inspectorate report on hospital discharge practices
in six areas acknowledged, the pressure to release hospital beds is
sometimes intense and caregivers have to respond to this (Department of
Health\SSI, 1995b, p. 27).

In the case of stroke patients, the caregivers concerned were told that
hospital care had to be rationed because beds were needed for other
patients:

> *I had to* [move him from the hospital]. *That was under the NHS rules.
> He could only stay in the stroke unit for 13 weeks. Then they moved him
> into a discharge unit. They said that 13 weeks was the limit and they
> needed his bed for somebody else. So he had to get out and go into this
> discharge unit.* (Wife)

When patients were Alzheimer sufferers, caregivers could be put under
enormous pressure to move them out of hospital at far shorter notice
because hospital staff found such patients difficult to cope with on a
medical ward. A wife who had coped with an increasingly confused

husband at home for several years was distressed because staff refused to keep him in hospital for observation after an accident:

They just didn't want him in there because he was obviously so confused and ... they hadn't really the facilities to handle confused people, it was as easy as that. So it meant that the doctor wanted him to come out regardless, he didn't care what happened to him, he just said, 'Get him out.' (Wife)

A son reported a similar experience. His mother who had lived by herself for several years was admitted to hospital as an emergency after collapsing because of an eating disorder. Staff insisted that she was too confused to remain:

There was no question of what we'd like to do. The consultant insisted that she leave hospital virtually that day with one day's notice and we were just staggered. (Son)

Although wives, daughters and sons were all equally likely to report feeling under pressure to move the cared-for person out of hospital, husbands looking after wives were the least likely to report feeling under pressure. Presumably staff were more likely to be sympathetic towards an elderly husband in a caring role than towards wives or daughters or sons. A second source of pressure reported by some family caregivers was the poor quality of care in the hospital. One son was outraged by the lack of attention to his mother:

I felt under pressure because the hospital care was so poor. Things were misdiagnosed and the nurses hung around eating chocolates. They ignored the patients.

A daughter distressed by her father's situation after a stroke tried to find a place in a nursing home because basic care in the hospital appeared so poor:

Yes there was pressure. They were so short-staffed I think. He wasn't cared for. When he needed changing or if he needed to go to the loo that wasn't done promptly. You could go there and he'd need changing. That wasn't

*very helpful for him or anybody else. He had to ask the staff to do
something about it. He needed cleaning up and that wasn't always done
very well. He was left to feed himself which he couldn't do. He would get
some help, I presume. But I would make a point of going in at tea-time so I
could feed him.*

Particular importance has been attached to developing effective hospital
discharge procedures between social services departments, health
authorities and hospitals under the 1990 NHS and Community Care Act.
But, as two Social Services Inspectorate inspections of hospital discharge
arrangements have shown, in many areas there are concerns about
hospital consultants either pre-judging the outcome of assessments or
pressurising for discharge (Department of Health/SSI, 1995a, 1995b).
When older people who have previously been supported in their own
homes enter care homes following a hospital discharge, the inevitable
question is whether appropriate rehabilitation might have enabled them
to return home. Little guidance based on research is currently available
as to the best approaches to rehabilitation (Medical Research Council,
1994). The Medical Research Council itself has called for an evaluation of
randomised trials of the effectiveness and cost-effectiveness of whole
packages of rehabilitation and of elements within community care
packages (Medical Research Council, 1994, p. 65). In evidence to the
House of Commons Health Committee on long-term care, the
Association of Directors of Social Services (1995/96a, p. 141) argued that
rehabilitation could create greater independence for older people and
reduce the demand for long-term institutional care. In addition the SSI
has been encouraging local authorities to consider developing short-stay
social rehabilitation schemes to enable older people to return to their
own homes after a stay in hospital instead of entering long-term care
(House of Commons Health Committee, 1995/96a, p. xix). Typically such
schemes based in adapted residential care homes allow an older person a
rehabilitation period of about six weeks after hospital discharge before
returning home.

As 60% of the cared-for people in the current study were reported to
have advanced dementia, rehabilitation may not have been feasible.
Although maintaining a cared-for person with dementia in the

community is of central importance to most family caregivers, the point is likely to be reached when it is neither in the caregiver's nor the dementia sufferer's interest to continue providing care at home. Using the OPCS survey of disability, Opit and Pahl (1993) developed a model for who would be most likely to be admitted to long-term institutional care. Key variables were a high degree of dependence, living alone and having dementia. It has been argued that certain community care policies such as closing down NHS geriatric beds will direct more people with dementia towards residential care because of the difficulties of sustaining them in the community (Sinclair, 1988; Netten, 1993).

Choosing a care home

Good practice guidance, as we have seen earlier in the chapter, emphasises the significance of frail elderly people making a positive choice to enter a care home. Research shows that older people are more likely to come to terms with admission if they themselves have exercised some degree of control over the choice to enter residential care (Weaver *et al.*, 1985). Several studies carried out before the implementation of the NHS and Community Care Act unanimously concluded that the initiative to enter a home was far more likely to lie with a relative or a professional rather than with the resident concerned (Neill *et al.*, 1988; Allen *et al.*, 1992; Phillips, 1992). A study of frail elderly people recently admitted to residential care in three local authorities, for example, reported only 22% saying that they themselves had taken the initiative to enter a care home; most reported that other people had made the initial suggestion (Allen *et al.*, 1992). The ability to make a choice in any area of life is enhanced by a basic understanding of the options available and by an individual's physical and mental fitness. A person who is physically dependent on others for the basic necessities in life inevitably has restricted choice. Although early or middle stage dementia may make it difficult to discuss choices; severe dementia may make it impossible. A family caregiver is likely to have reservations about attempting to talk over the options with a dementia sufferer because of the communication problems and the emotional conflict often accompanying caring for somebody with this illness. A practical guide to understanding dementia suggested that relatives often prefer to leave a professional person to attempt communicating the options to the person with dementia. This can result in serious misunderstanding, particularly when admission to a care home is one of the options under discussion (Murphy, 1986).

Two out of three cared-for people were admitted to a care home from hospital, a factor that further circumscribed the choices available. As a Social Services Inspectorate report on hospital discharge arrangements commented, for many older people discharged from hospital, finding an appropriate care home is complicated by their frailty, vulnerability and grief at not being able to return to their own homes (Department of Health\SSI, 1995b, p. 25). Central to older people choosing or agreeing to enter a care home is the F (fear) factor – fear of falling, fear of attack, fear of being unable to cope and general anxiety (Department of Health, 1994a).

What choices were available?

Good practice guidance emphasises not only the importance of making a 'positive choice' to enter a care home, but also the importance of being able to choose between different homes; to quote from SSI guidance on care home standards:

> *Furthermore, a 'good' home will have been selected from a range of options as an informed choice by the resident, with involvement of relatives and other advisers as appropriate to his or her ability to exercise choice.*
> (Department of Health\SSI, 1990 p. 15)

As in other studies, it was clear that most family caregivers choose the care home and few potential residents actually visited one prior to admission. Many factors restrict the choices that can be made and cost remains a significant restriction. If the cared-for person or caregiver cannot afford to top up a local authority baseline fee, then a care home charging the right price must be found and in some areas this may be particularly difficult. A second restriction is the current availability of places in residential or nursing homes. Family caregivers will find it far more difficult to find a vacant care home place in some areas than in others. There are wide regional variations in the availability of care home places. The highest concentration of private residential homes is to be found in the South and South West, where local authority provision is low (Laing and Buisson, 1996). The nursing home sector which developed later than the residential home sector has expanded most rapidly outside these traditional areas. The regions of highest nursing home concentration are now in the North and the Midlands. Taking all forms of institutional provision together, Greater London has the lowest number of beds in relation to the age adjusted population, at 61% of the UK average (Laing and Buisson, 1996, p. 62).

A third restriction on choice is most family caregivers' lack of any previous experience of either residential or nursing homes. Most respondents recalled that when they set out to find a suitable care home they had no idea what to expect.

I don't know, I'd never been in one before. (Daughter)

I had no idea about it really. (Son)

I don't think I had any idea really because it wasn't relevant. It wasn't a concern. (Wife)

When people recalled having views these were largely negative:

I thought they were places where people went to die. (Daughter)

Well I imagined it either as people sitting around, almost in a state of being in a coma, or just walking round like zombies. (Daughter)

More like a kind of glorified workhouse. (Son)

A small number of respondents did have some idea about care homes either because they had already visited somebody in one or through their work. With such limited and negative preconceptions of care homes, however, most family caregivers had little or no basis for making choices between different types of care homes. Caregivers were asked if they had ever previously discussed the possibility of entering a care home with the cared-for person. Most were emphatic that there had been no prior discussion because the last thing wanted had been the cared-for person's admission to a care home. Even to have raised the possibility would have been interpreted as a rejection. A fourth restriction was home owners' or managers' preferences as they are in a powerful position to offer or to withhold an available place. A study of the admission process to private residential care homes carried out before the implementation of the 1990 NHS and Community Care Act (which included interviews with 200 residents) in Suffolk reported that home owners appeared to be particularly significant in the selection process by exercising a role in gatekeeping and assessment (Phillips, 1992). Although it is difficult to gauge the influence of managers or owners in a retrospective study, it was in evidence. Several caregivers felt that a care home place had been secured because they had managed to convince the manager that a parent or spouse would fit in with other residents in the care home.

Under the 1984 Registered Homes Act owners or managers are required to produce brochure prospectuses describing the faculties and policies. Interestingly only about half the family caregivers thought they had seen any written information about individual care homes before an admission had been arranged. The SSI review of hospital discharge arrangements also drew attention to a lack of available written information: 'the range and quality of information available to assist in choosing a home is often inadequate and where it does exist patients and their families often fail to get what is available' (Department of Health\SSI, 1995b, p. 3). Social services departments can help a cared-for person and family caregiver make the right choice, by giving information, and by helping to arrange visits. Individual social workers themselves have considerable scope in how helpful or otherwise they are to people and, of course, in what they actually say about individual homes. Four different scenarios were apparent in the processes of selecting an individual care home:

- a social worker chose the home and made the placement

- caregivers made their own arrangements

- caregivers were given a restricted list of a small number of homes

- caregivers were given a complete list of all the homes in the area.

A social worker chose the home and made the placement

A social worker was reported to have chosen a suitable care home in a small number of cases without the family caregiver concerned visiting it before the placement. All those concerned were spouses in their eighties who had spent several years caring for a partner with dementia at home. On the whole they expressed relief that a social worker had taken the process over and sorted out a suitable nursing home:

> *Jim [the social worker] said, 'It's alright, it's a nice place, five-star hotel'. He said, 'Let's transfer her'. I said, 'Well you seem to like it, when you authorise it she can move'.* (Husband)

> *The social worker worked all that out. I never took part in that sort of thing. I agreed that she could go in like. I said, 'If you think that she won't manage at home it's got to be one or the other'. They done all that.* (Husband)

> *They did it for me.* (Wife)

Virtually all those who had had no direct involvement in choosing a care home were husbands. The wife who was the one exception was 85 years old and had looked after a husband suffering from both Parkinson's disease and dementia for five years. When her husband became very aggressive and would no longer allow her to leave the flat for even a brief time to go shopping, she herself suffered a nervous breakdown and her husband was admitted temporarily to a local authority residential home. The day before her husband was due to be discharged from the local authority home, the social worker suggested two possible private residential homes but:

> *When we visited the first one they'd no room. So this other one, where he is now, we called in there, and I think they'd about three places there, three rooms. She took me round to see the bedroom that he'd fancy. There was about three vacant rooms and I chose the one that I thought would be suitable for him. It was roomy, and a nice bed and a wardrobe, and a set of drawers and things like that. And so I chose that.*

Caregivers made their own arrangements
Some caregivers had very definite ideas of the care home wanted and made their own arrangements. In almost all cases placements were made in a home specifically for people of a particular religious denomination. Several considerations appeared to have been taken into account such as specific customs and diet that would be familiar to the cared-for person. An additional factor for the family caregivers involved was the assumption that a care home run by a religious organisation would be of a higher standard than one run by a secular organisation. Another factor made explicit by some of these caregivers was that the cared-for person's admission to a specific religious denomination care home was less damaging to their own reputation as a caring responsible person than an admission to a secular home. As one of the daughters commented:

> *The reason we chose a care home run by* [name of religious organisation] *was so that my father could hold up his head with his friends.*

Caregivers were given a list of care homes
Social workers in some of the areas in the study did not give out complete lists but suggested three or four likely homes. Sometimes these were the homes with current vacancies but more often this was not the case and caregivers ended up going back to social services for more suggestions or found other ways to locate care homes.

The most common procedure for both spouses and adult children was being given a list of all homes in an area. Often this list was not accompanied by advice about individual homes:

> *They gave me a list and I went to see about seven. I asked for their advice but they said they were not allowed to give it, they said it was up to me to select one. This was about the best.* (Son)

Such an absence of service-based information to assist people in making choices about placements was noted in the SSI report on the national inspection of discharge arrangements from hospital to care homes (Department of Health\SSI, 1995a).

Sometimes social workers did help directly. One daughter reported that she found a care home she liked but it had no vacancies. While expressing a preference for it to the social worker she had to keep on looking. Eventually the social worker telephoned a warning that a vacancy was imminent because one of the residents was dying. By telephoning the matron concerned again the daughter was able to get her mother into a care home place by jumping the waiting list.

Some caregivers were able to utilise a list and set about choosing a care home in the same way that a well-informed consumer would make any major purchase. Appointments were made to view individual care homes, staff were cross-questioned about the quality of life in the home and residents' lounges were observed. At the extreme, a few caregivers had managed to visit more than 20 care homes. Most caregivers interviewed, however, were not able to exercise choice in this way. They were intimidated by the whole process. As many as half the spouses and one in three of the adult children had only ever visited the one home in which the placement was actually made. This lack of shopping around seemed to occur for several reasons. The commonest was that a placement had to be sorted out swiftly because of the pressure to move the cared-for person out of hospital. Some of the frailer spouses were railroaded by the speed of the decision. For example, one of the wives in her late eighties whose husband had suffered a major stroke experienced a discussion about a possible care home on one day and an actual placement the following day:

> *It was so quick. Mr* [the consultant] *came down and saw me and he said, 'I think we had better get him in a place. Where would you like him to go?' I said, '[Name of home]'. So the next day I had a phone call to say there was a vacancy and the matron would be coming to see me. Then she rang up and said he could go straight there and then the next day when I went to the hospital he was gone.*

One of the daughters, informed that her mother had to be discharged from hospital the following day, was given no choice:

That was the only place available. There wasn't any choice, she either had to go there or it would have been coming home, and the psychiatrist who saw her, that we met, said that she couldn't possibly cope on her own.

Another reason for not shopping around was failing to understand the system. Social workers appeared to assume that caregivers would work through a list and would realise that they had to contact homes directly. Several respondents reported being bemused by the situation. A daughter complained:

I think the social services could have sat us down and said, 'This is what you need to do. These are the people you need to approach. These are the things you're entitled to claim.' We'd never done that before. My father just dropped dead. So we never had all that and my husband's parents have been dead for many, many years. It was the first time we'd ever come across this. We weren't even told which homes we could actually choose from. They just said, 'You go round. It's up to you now. If you want to put her in a home you go and do it.'

It is likely that some caregivers had been given comprehensive information but had failed to grasp what had been said because their stress levels were so high. A few caregivers had wanted to visit several care homes but had been denied the opportunity. One of the daughters helping her father find a suitable place for a mother with severe dementia was very upset when an admissions officer for the organisation concerned said there was no point in visiting any of the organisation's homes because there was no way of knowing in which one a vacancy might occur.

In a few instances there had been no choice because the cared-for person had to be moved out of one care home when staff were unable to handle disruptive behaviour. A placement had to be accepted in the only local home willing to cope with a parent's behaviour.

For some caregivers, however, only looking at one care home was a positive choice because it seemed so desirable:

No. Once we had seen it that was it. (Daughter)

I only wanted her to go there, it's a Christian home and I had known it ever since childhood. (Daughter-in-law)

Factors influencing choice

Two significant factors influencing caregivers were location and atmosphere. A desirable care home had to be within reasonable travelling distance. When there was access to a car, as most daughters and sons had, then ten miles might seem reasonable. But, if a caregiver relied on public transport or taxis, as did most spouses, then a care home within two or three miles was preferred. As spouses tended to visit very frequently the question of location became crucial.

It was not easy to understand what caregivers really meant by the right atmosphere. For some it seemed to mean the absence of an authoritarian regime:

When we went down to view it, we just liked the atmosphere. The atmosphere was very, very easy. No strict regime at all. They were very, sort of open. I felt that the place was lovely and bright. (Daughter)

For others pleasant wallpaper and curtains were important:

It was a nice atmosphere. They've got it nice. Well I know you don't go for the decor really, but it does help doesn't it? (Daughter)

Certain caregivers emphasised the importance of cleanliness and tidiness. One of the husbands commented:

Well, when I went to look really I was shown round it and, well you don't know the staff obviously, but I mean it was all spick and span and everything looked well. I thought, 'You can't better this.'

Some people trying to find a suitable place for an Alzheimer sufferer looked for something to make that person feel at home. One of the wives chose a home with pets knowing her husband's fondness for animals:

We went to all the residential homes around the area to see what they were like. My son and I talked it over afterwards to decide whether we thought

*they were right or not and in most cases they just weren't right for Dad.
So we had to just put him in what we thought was the favourite one
because of the dogs.*

Various indicators were seen as important to good quality care.
Cleanliness, the absence of incontinence smells, flourishing gardens with
trees and flowers, pleasant care assistants were all mentioned as
significant. Although there is no consensus about what form of
residential care is most appropriate for dementia sufferers there is a
debate about how a care home could best be organised. Should dementia
sufferers be integrated with mentally able residents or should they be in
homes exclusively for dementia sufferers? Is it better for dementia
sufferers to be in a large home with communal facilities or is it better to
have small group living units? Caregivers of dementia sufferers seemed
largely unaware of these possible options. Interestingly only one
respondent mentioned choosing a care home with small group living
units because she felt that sitting in a large communal lounge would
have only added to her mother's feeling of confusion.

In conclusion

There has been increasing government and professional commitment to
giving family caregivers and those who are being cared for greater
choice. Integral to any notion of choice is that there should be a range
from which to choose and the power or opportunity to make a choice.
The pressures on spouses is likely to be different from the pressures on
sons and daughters. This study confirmed the findings of other studies,
that those being cared for by spouses in the community were far more
dependent at the point when community care came to an end than those
being cared for by daughters or sons. Wives had a particularly heavy
caring burden and yet were least likely to receive support services.

An appropriate package of care when people need intensive personal
attention is problematic to organise. Some of the descriptions of care
assistants arriving either very late in the morning or very early in the
evening to assist the cared-for person in getting up or going to bed made
it clear that, when this kind of support is not available at appropriate
times, it is itself another source of stress.

Two-thirds of the caregiving situations in the community had come to an end when the cared-for person entered hospital. Many of the family caregivers concerned felt that they had been pressurised into moving their relative out of hospital and into long-term care. If short-stay rehabilitation had been available locally, it is possible that some of those admitted to a care home could have eventually returned to their own homes.

Few family caregivers had any previous experience of care homes. On the whole they did not know what to expect or what to look for. As we shall see in the following chapter, at the beginning of the process few had any idea of how a care home is paid for. Although some caregivers made their own arrangements for a particular care home or shopped around extensively to find a care home of good quality, most were intimidated by the situation. Because there is little knowledge in the general population about care homes, many of the caregivers in the sample needed advice and support. When people do not understand what the choices are, they are not properly equipped to exercise the right to choose. For many caregivers in the sample, little choice had been evident anyway because placements had to be made fast and vacancies were few and far between.

Financial consequences of an admission to a care home for family caregivers

Introduction

This chapter focuses on the costs to family caregivers of an older person's admission to long-term residential or nursing home care. Financial consequences are likely for family caregivers as well as the individual concerned. If a person has previously been dependent in the community and supported by family members, an admission to long-term care may involve some savings on the costs to them. The chapter begins by examining some of the care costs to family caregivers when the cared-for person lived at home. It then focuses on what caregivers recollected knowing about the current system of paying for residential or nursing home care before the cared-for person's admission. The chapter then explores the position of spouses who, as legally liable relatives, can be directly charged for care home costs. Additional costs in care homes to both spouses and offspring are then discussed. The chapter concludes by looking at the impact of the current charging policies on the future inheritance prospects of the family caregivers in the sample.

Savings on care costs in the community

With the exception of people who had suffered a stroke and become dependent overnight, those now in residential care homes had previously needed considerable support in the community. Family caregivers were asked about statutory or private support services in the community that had been utilised. Estimates were made of weekly costs for any service. Questions were also asked about other kinds of costs such as heating or transport. Collecting information about retrospective costs is inevitably problematic. In the present study it was further complicated by the passage of time. The mean length of time since the cared-for person had lived at home was 18 months. Although some had entered a few months before the interview, others had been admitted as much as two or three years earlier. Differences were apparent between family caregivers in their involvement in the cared-for person's finances. Co-residence as in the case of spouses usually meant that costs were met from joint incomes. Although some daughters and sons living in different households had little idea of what the parent paid for services, others kept a close eye on charges. Inevitably these costs can be discussed only in fairly broad terms. The different types of costs described included:

- direct expenditure on goods or services

- non-waged time

- waged time.

Direct expenditure on goods or services
Approximately half the cared-for people now in a care home were reported to have had some support from the statutory services while living in the community. As we have seen in the previous chapter, daughters and sons were more likely than spouses to report support from the statutory services. Assistance with bathing was the most frequently mentioned type of support. Few spouses reported having had help with cleaning, but more than a third of the daughters and sons reported that their parents had had a home help. Relatively few cared-for people were reported to have purchased assistance from private sources.

Although local authorities have to implement a national scheme for charging for residential or nursing home care, they do not have to charge for domiciliary services. Under Section 17 of the Health and Social Services Adjudication and Social Security Adjudication Act (HASSASSA) 'an authority providing a service may recover such charge (if any) for it as they consider reasonable' (S.17 (1)). Most authorities now make charges and the level of charges has been rising (Secretary of State for Health, 1996, B.13). The basis of charging varies, with some services (particularly meals-on-wheels) charged for at a flat rate and others at differential rates (related to the level of service provided and the income of the service user). National figures indicate that service users meet 10%

of the total cost of day and domiciliary services (Secretary of State for Health, 1996, A. 18).

Not all the family caregivers in the sample could remember what if anything had been charged for services. When they could remember, the amounts were relatively modest for statutory services. A mean charge of £14.11 per week to the service user was estimated in contrast to the mean charge for private services of £97.14 per week. A person living alone but finding it difficult to manage living independently in the community is likely to be meeting many direct costs personally. Only a few daughters and sons living in a different household from a parent reported personally paying for goods or services. One of the daughters paid for her mother's home care assistant and meals-on-wheels and another did all her mother's shopping and paid for it out of her own pocket. A son reported that his wife took a cooked dinner round to his mother every evening but there had never been any charge for the food. Another son rather vaguely described himself as meeting many of the bills sent to his mother out of his own pocket. But costs could be high and regular. One of the sons, for example, living in a separate household from his mother, a dementia sufferer, reported being asked to contribute towards his mother's extensive package of care. Several care assistants provided 24-hour cover for five days and nights of the week sleeping in the mother's flat. A different son provided cover for two days of the week. The respondent agreed to purchase the week's shopping for his mother and the team of care assistants and to meet heating costs in the flat. The amount of money paid out obviously varied each week but the son remembered it as a considerable expense.

Co-residence generally seemed to result in a higher expenditure to a family caregiver than if the cared-for person lived in a separate household. Sharing a household means that payment of direct costs may be met by anyone in the household or a combination of any or all household members. Extra expenditure over and above the normal cost of living described by the caregiver included goods such as heating or food, and services such as home care or meals-on-wheels. The three daughters whose mothers had previously lived with them described particularly high expenditure on items such as heating. Central heating had to be run constantly as the mothers rarely left the house. All three reported being reluctant to ask the parent for a realistic contribution to household expenses. One woman whose mother lived with her for two-and-a-half years before being admitted to a care home commented:

The thing I notice most is that I no longer spend so much on heating and food. She only ever paid me £15 a week.

High heating bills were also mentioned by several spouses. One husband, for example, described his wife, a dementia sufferer, as always getting up very early in the morning and putting on all the fires in the house. Telephone bills could be another source of high expenditure. Two of the husbands described wives with dementia constantly telephoning at all times of the day and night. One man estimated that the cost was about £50 per week.

Until recently local authorities have had the power to charge a service user but not the power to assess or charge either adult children or partners or spouses directly. A DH note to the SSI, however, has recently opened up this issue: 'Local authorities may, in individual cases wish to consider whether a client has sufficient reliable access to resources beyond those held in his/her name for them to be part of his/her means for the purposes of section 17(3)' (i.e. HASSASS) (quoted in Fimister, 1995). Only a few respondents had been asked to pay some of the care costs by a local authority. The son who had had to meet the food and heating costs for a small team of care assistants has already been described in this chapter. The previous chapter also described a wife deciding she could no longer cope with looking after her husband at home when the local authority estimated a charge to her of £200 a week to meet the costs of a relatively modest package of care.

One of six key objectives set out in the white paper 'Caring for People' was to make proper assessment of need and good care management the cornerstone of high quality care: 'the packages of care should be designed in line with individual needs and preferences' (Secretaries of State for Health, Social Security, Wales and Scotland, 1989). The Association of County Councils in evidence to the House of Commons Health Committee on long-term care, however, made it clear that it is now widespread practice for local authorities to limit the cost of domiciliary care packages to the cost of a place in a residential care home (House of Commons Health Committee, 1995/96b, Q.680).

Non-waged time

As in other studies comparing the caregiving experiences of adult children and spouses, on both sides of the Atlantic, there can be no doubt that, on the whole, spouses were looking after people who were more dependent and needed more help with personal care (Wenger, 1984; Townsend, 1990). They were also more likely than daughters or sons to meet those needs themselves and less likely to be supported by formal services. Wives were particularly likely to experience a heavy caring burden and were the least likely to have support from the statutory services. What most spouses had in common was that they spent large amounts of time in caregiving. Not surprisingly a common point was for spouses to feel unable to continue in a caregiving role when it became impossible to have any time at all away from the person being cared for.

Although several of the daughters interviewed lived in a separate household from the parent, they found it difficult to lead an independent life because of going to the parent's house several times during the day and often during the evening as well. One of the daughters aged 72 had only gained some independence two years earlier when her mother had been admitted to a care home at the age of 99. For ten years before admission her mother had refused all social services support insisting, 'My daughter does all that for me'. During those ten years her daughter had been unable to have even a day away because of the need to attend her mother several times each day:

> Oh it's been a lot better since she's been up there. I'm able to get up in the mornings and say, 'Oh we'll go out today'. But I couldn't do that when I'd got her. She would not have anybody else in the house to do things for her so I had to do her meals and her shopping and her cleaning. Even when she was down her own little home, you'd always got that feeling – is she all right? I always used to say to her, 'Now don't answer that door. Whatever you do don't answer the door.' Well you get people knocking on

the door and then she'd be on the phone saying, 'There's somebody at the door and I don't know who it is'. So I would end up having to run down there.

Waged time
Several daughters but none of the sons had given up paid employment because of a parent's need for care. One daughter, for example, had given up a full-time job because she was summoned to her father's house at various points in the day and night as he panicked at being on his own. All those who had given up jobs had managed to go back to work after a parent's admission to a care home. Caregiving had long-term financial consequences which affected caregivers after caring had ceased. If caregivers give up employment, they may find it difficult to find another job, or may have to take a lower paid one. Pensions are likely to be reduced in retirement because without paid employment people are unlikely to be able to pay into occupational or state schemes. The impact that caregiving has on employment is well established. A re-analysis of a government retirement survey reported that 14% of men and 25% of women had had their working lives affected in some way by caregiving (Hancock and Jarvis, 1994). They had either lost a job, taken a lower paid job, had difficulty getting a job or lost pay because of their caring responsibilities.

Previous knowledge of the system of paying for care

As Chapter 2 describes, in reality there are two systems for meeting long-term care home costs; one when there is a surviving spouse, and the other when a person is single or widowed. Spouses are considered liable relatives and may be asked to contribute towards care costs. A house lived in by a spouse, however, should not be taken into account. Adult children are not considered liable relatives but, if the person entering a care home has lived alone and has been an owner occupier, the value of a house will be taken into account. In both circumstances, an individual's savings are taken into account and if higher than £16,000 an individual would meet full care home costs.

Respondents were asked what they had known about paying for care in a residential or nursing home before the cared-for person's admission. Some caregivers said they understood that there would be means-testing and payment would be a mixture of state funding and personal income and savings. Many spouses and offspring, however, reported that right up to admission they thought that a place in a care home would be free and paid for by the NHS.

> *I actually thought everything was paid for on the National Health. I didn't know anything about it. I never really gave it a thought to be honest.* (Daughter)

> *At one stage I should imagine I thought it was all part of the health service. It was a bit of a shock to find it wasn't.* (Husband)

> *I actually thought everything was paid for on the National Health. I didn't know anything about it.* (Son)

Why did so many family caregivers apparently fail to investigate or comprehend the financial implications of an admission to a care home? Three interrelated factors appeared as: a lack of accessible information, the complexity of the system and family caregivers' own emotional blocks to seeking out relevant information.

Lack of accessible information

Although several respondents were appreciative of the time and effort an individual social worker had taken during an assessment process to explain the complexities of the current charging system, a surprising number of respondents maintained that they had only really found out about it after the cared-for person's admission to a care home. Several caregivers reported that they had only begun to understand the income and savings implications after the care home manager concerned had spent time in going into all the details:

> *Mrs* [name of matron] *the matron is marvellous. She takes you in and explains everything to you.*

Caregivers could become very upset on discovering that savings would be taken into account. One of the daughters, for example, reported that she discovered the rules only several months after her mother had entered the care home:

I thought because of talking to a friend some years ago that when you got admitted to a home they just took your pension book. The home took the book and they paid for everything out of the book. I assumed that's what you had to do because once she was admitted nobody told us any different. We found everything out by error.

Because of administrative delays, several months passed before the local authority presented the daughter with a bill for £2,000. At this point the daughter, in a state of total panic, discovered her mother's eligibility for income support. But the Benefits Agency was reported as refusing to backdate payments and the family itself had to meet this initial bill.

Other research shows that local authorities are often poor at transmitting information to service users. A study of local authority charging policies for community care, for example, concluded that both staff and service users lacked information on policies and users' rights (Baldwin and Lunt, 1996).

Complexities and inequities in the current system
Family caregivers do not, in reality, experience an equitable system with national rules and policies. Spouse liability in particular is interpreted in different ways both by individual local authorities and by individual social workers within one authority. Although there is a statutory liability, a spouse's declaration of income is voluntary. Some local authorities, however, routinely send a spouse remaining in the community an income declaration form. It may never be made clear that there is no obligation to complete it. One of the husbands, for example, himself a professional person who had consulted widely about charges for care, was intimidated when the local authority sent him a form to complete before his wife with advanced dementia was admitted to a nursing home:

I got one or two guidelines from the care manager, but the people who were most helpful to me were Age Concern. Of that there is no doubt. They sent me all the paraphernalia, what to do and where to go and what not to do. And I studied it all, I was still somewhat uncertain as to what my position was in it. But it seemed unclear as to what I was expected to contribute, until finally we came down to the nitty-gritty of applying for financial aid, if you like, I got this massive form from social services ... which asked for both my earnings and my savings and my wife's earnings and savings. I got back onto the local Age Concern Office and the worker said, 'Ignore what they are asking from you because they do not need it. All they need to know is your wife's finances. Put that down and ignore everything else.'

Several spouses reported being stopped by a social worker from declaring their own savings. A wife, for example, revealed to a social worker that she had recently inherited a relatively large sum of money and was told that he would pretend that she had not told him. One of the husbands had a similar experience:

I said to the social worker, 'Will I pay towards her there?' and he said, 'No you don't want to do that', and he put a cross through that question.

Another complexity frequently misunderstood is the right to an attendance, or disability living, allowance if paying privately. A resident is no longer eligible for an attendance allowance if a local authority accepts financial responsibility. If a resident is self-funding, however, an attendance allowance may be paid. Several daughters and sons reported a parent assessed as needing care by a local authority but being told that savings were currently too high for public funding. No advice was given during the assessment process about the parent's eligibility for an attendance allowance as a self-funder. Part of family caregivers' exasperation on discovering eligibility months later was the discovery that an attendance allowance is not back-dated. If the parent had been awarded the attendance allowance earlier, savings would have been run down more slowly. Other misunderstandings about the attendance allowance emerged. An 85 year old wife reported that nobody had explained that her husband could no longer claim an attendance allowance after being admitted to a care home with local authority funding. She was grateful for the continued attendance allowance because it met the cost of the taxis necessary for her to reach the care home. Eventually the local Benefits Agency discovered that she had been overpaid £800. At the point she was interviewed it was being repaid at the rate of £4 per week.

Emotional blocks to comprehension

Although the sheer complexity of the system is a barrier to understanding how care is paid for, it is far from being the only one. After years of coping at home some caregivers were so stressed that they found it difficult to comprehend what was being explained either about care homes or about payment. Spouses, themselves often frail and in their eighties, were particularly likely to be overwhelmed. For example, one of the wives recollected:

I really didn't grasp how it was paid for. I was going through a very bad patch, with him going into a home anyway, and I'd been up to the doctor's and I'd collapsed up there and made a fool of myself and all the rest of it, and I was on tranquillisers to try and steady me up. All I knew was that if we had any money at all, then we were going to have to pay.

Dazed by his wife going into a care home, a husband was unable to grasp what he should do and was only too willing to co-operate with social services:

The care managers came down and took details of what we had and savings and what-not and – it went on this year – it was a bit less last year. No but they did virtually everything for me as regards to applying for the community tax. I didn't have a clue really what was going on.

In effect many of the husbands and wives interviewed admitted that not only had they not understood the complexities of the system initially, they had remained confused:

She [the social worker] *did actually explain things quite well. But, because to be honest, with all the pressures that were on us at the time I'm not really sure that I took it all in. Certainly going back on it now I'm still slightly confused as to who is paying what. I still actually don't know to what extent we are receiving any other subsidy other than income support. I just don't know. I've tried to find out.* (Wife)

Spouse caregivers were likely to be very reluctant to contemplate a partner's admission to a care home until it proved impossible to continue providing care at home. Finding out either about care homes or paying for them before the crisis would have been considered disloyal to the cared-for person.

Well I'd never considered it. I'd never thought about it really as it happens. (Wife)

I didn't give it a thought really. It didn't affect me. I never thought it would come to me. (Husband)

By the end some family caregivers had become so overwhelmed by their situation and so desperate to get the cared-for person into a care home that finding out about costs became immaterial:

I thought it was me. Everyone was saying to me – in fact friends were saying, 'Have you got to pay for it?' I said, 'I don't know yet. I'd like to get her in first and worry about the money afterwards.' (Daughter)

I thought the Government would pay for the home which you do I suppose. You're naive about everything. Really I was so relieved to get him in there I didn't realise how you would pay or anything until the letters started coming through. You don't realise, do you? (Wife)

Current understanding of the system of paying for care
Not surprisingly, given their distress and being overwhelmed by the financial complexities of an admission to a care home, several wives had handed pensions, bank accounts and bills over to a son or a daughter's management. A wife who spent virtually every waking moment in a nursing home at her husband's side had no idea whether she paid for meals eaten at the home or whether there were any extra charges of any kind. Her response to questions about costs were:

I don't know anything about that. My son does it all for me. My life is finished. I will see him [her husband] *out and then die myself.*

Family caregivers tended to be particularly confused about two aspects of current policies: one was specific to spouses and related to the treatment of a couple's property and the other, affecting all family caregivers, was the rules in respect of capital limits on savings.

The treatment of a couple's property

Although the value of a house must be taken into account if a resident lived alone before admission to a care home, a local authority must ignore the value of a property if a spouse is living in it (see Chapter 2). The situation is not so straightforward if the spouse remaining in the community decides to sell the matrimonial home and buy a smaller property. Department of Social Security guidance makes it clear that a resident's share in the matrimonial home should be ignored:

> *At the time the property is sold, the resident's 50% share of the proceeds could be taken into account in the charging assessment but, in order to enable the spouse to purchase the smaller property, the resident makes part of his share of the proceeds from the sale available to the spouse. In these circumstances, in the Department's view, it would not be reasonable for the resident to have to deprive himself of capital in order to reduce his residential accommodation charge.* (Department of Social Security, 1995b, par. 6.063)

Many spouse caregivers interviewed who were owner occupiers had a very different understanding of their rights in respect of property. They believed that a local authority had placed a charge against the matrimonial home and that, regardless of whether the partner in the care home or the partner in the community died first, the property would eventually be forfeit to the local authority. These views were reinforced by relatives, friends, the media, local authority employees and even welfare rights organisations. Other Joseph Rowntree Foundation funded research makes it clear that local authority policies in respect of charging for community support services are frequently misunderstood both by service users and the local authority employees administering the system (Baldwin and Lunt, 1996). Inaccuracies in respect of the treatment of property are often conveyed to clients by local authority employees when implementing charging policies for social care (Meredith, 1995a).

Some respondents had personal experience of local authority treatment of property rights that contravened national guidelines. A husband in his eighties, whose wife had entered a nursing home, wanted to move to a smaller flat. He reported that a local authority social worker had advised him that the local authority would claim any capital difference between the property sold and the property bought. This advice was confirmed by an independent local welfare rights worker:

> *There's no point in me leaving here because as the law stands once the partner has gone into residential care they don't turf the spouse out. But in the event of me or anyone else leaving this house then they take the proceeds. I got in touch with the local Citizens' Advice Bureau – they had a look at it for me and they said that's how the law stood.*

One of the wives, in her late fifties, had directly experienced a local authority successfully claiming the capital difference when she sold a large house to move to a small flat. Mrs B had looked after her husband who had advanced multiple sclerosis for several years at home. Eventually when he had become doubly incontinent and unable to move himself in any way, the physical and mental strain became too much and she had a nervous breakdown. Mr B was admitted to a nursing home following a local authority assessment. As this occurred before the new rules were introduced in April 1996, her husband's whole substantial occupational pension had been taken by the local authority and she had been advised to apply for income support. In order to have more money to live on Mrs B decided to sell her large house and buy a small property. Not only had local authority officials stepped in and insisted that half the capital released had to be paid over towards the cost of her husband's care, they had objected to the amount she spent refurbishing the new property because it reduced the amount of capital released to the local authority by the sale.

When CRAG (Charging for Residential Accommodation Guidance) rules are interpreted in this way (as they clearly are being in some areas) it is not surprising that spouse caregivers remaining in the community believe that a local authority has a right to their property. Nevertheless, it must be a common reaction for a spouse whose partner has been admitted to long-term care to want to move house. This may seem desirable for all sorts of reasons. The spouses concerned are often themselves of an advanced age and getting frailer and a smaller property is likely to be both cheaper and easier to maintain. Emotional reasons for wanting to move would include the matrimonial home being a depressing reminder of the absent partner and a failure to cope with providing care at home. A spouse moving into a care home is after all a change in marital status equivalent to a death or a divorce. Re-analyses of GHS data showed a relationship between moving home and changed marital status, i.e. death or divorce is likely to lead to greater levels of change of residence (Askham *et al.*, 1992, Figure 3.3).

Failure to understand capital limit rules
Two aspects of capital limits appeared to be misunderstood by local authority employees and family caregivers alike. The first was the actual level of the capital limits. These were raised on 1 April 1996. The lower limit below which savings are totally disregarded was raised from £3,000 to £10,000 and the upper limit raised from £8,000 to £16,000. Some charges are made on savings between the lower and an upper limit (see Chapter 2 for details). The second was the rules in respect of a couple's savings. When a resident's savings are being used to pay part of the costs, family caregivers often rely on care managers who originally recorded all the financial details to inform them about the rules regarding joint savings and, if contributions have to be paid, when savings have been reduced to the permitted limits. But such trust may be mistaken. Evidently care managers may be just as confused as caregivers about how a courple's savings should be treated.

Under income support rules, when a couple lives at home in the community, the capital held by both spouses will be added together and treated in the same way as the capital held by a single person (Benefits Agency, 1996, p. 144). But, if one person permanently enters a residential care or nursing home, both partners can claim support separately (Benefits Agency, 1996, p. 71). If there are joint savings, half of these should be declared as belonging to the resident (Age Concern England, 1996b).

Although local authority officials collect financial information, there appears to be no mechanism to notify relatives when savings have been reduced to the limits. Mistakes were made with individual savings limits as well as limits for joint savings. For example, one of the daughters interviewed several months after capital limits were introduced with a minimum limit of £10,000 was still paying each month from her mother's savings towards care costs despite them being down to £4,000.

Mr Rogers' wife who was an Alzheimer's disease sufferer had been admitted to a residential home after being looked after at home for several years. When she was admitted to a care home the couple had joint savings of £11,000. At this point the minimum limit for a resident was £3,000 and the maximum £8,000. The care manager told Mr Rogers he would have to pay full charges. Two months after his wife had been admitted, the limits for a person in a residential or nursing home changed to £10,000 minimum and £16,000 maximum. Income support limits for a person living in the community remained the same. When interviewed Mr Rogers reported that £7,000 had been paid from joint savings to the local authority and that only £4,000 was left. He was still paying £200 per week towards his wife's care and assumed that the care manager would tell him when savings were spent down to the limit.

The costs of long-term care to family caregivers

An admission to a care home is likely to have financial consequences of some kind for family caregivers. The nature of these consequences depends in part on the relationship with the person who has been admitted. As liable relatives, spouses could be charged by a local authority for part or all of the costs but adult children do not have a statutory liability for their parents. Five broad categories of costs were discernible:

- direct costs to spouses

- topping up local authority payments

- extra costs in the care home

- caregiver additional costs

- loss of a future inheritance.

Direct costs to spouses
A couple's income and savings will be affected by the admission of one partner to a care home. Inevitably pensions will be cut. A couple's state retirement pension will be spilt in halves leaving the person remaining in the community with a pension worth considerably less than a single person in similar circumstances would receive. Before April 1996, someone entering care was generally required to put all of her or his occupational pension towards the cost of that care (see Chapter 2). As a husband was more likely than a wife to have an occupational pension, this ruling often meant considerable hardship for wives when husbands were admitted to care because the household income would fall by the amount of the occupational pension. Since April 1996 this problem was addressed by introducing an occupational pension disregard. Half of a married resident's occupational pension must be ignored providing that at least half the pension is being paid to a spouse remaining in the community (Secretary of State for Health, 1996, par. B).

Several wives whose husbands had been admitted to care before April 1996 had lost the whole occupational pension (although half the pension had been payable to them since that date). They had been forced to claim income support for the first time in order to survive financially. This could be a tremendous shock. One of the wives concerned described her devastation at being rendered virtually destitute when her husband was admitted to a nursing home after years of being cared for at home:

They said to me, 'You can get income support'. I didn't know what income support was. I'd heard of it vaguely. That was for people who had no money at all. But John had worked all his life. He had a salary and a pension. What's income support got to do with it? It didn't add up to me that I should go on income support because John was ill. I always thought his pension was there to provide for both of us. I can't find words to describe what I feel about it. Initially it just broke me up – I had to walk away from it. I had to go to a psychiatric ward. It wasn't just the money. It was just the whole degrading and undignified way it was handled. No compassion at all.

Several wives but none of the husbands described the period after the cared-for person had been admitted to a care home as financial chaos. As far as the wives were concerned if the husband had been admitted to a care home before April 1996 there had been the loss of the whole of the husband's occupational pension. If the admission had occurred since April 1996 half the pension was still taken. But as far as the husbands whose wives had entered a care home were concerned, there was rarely an occupational pension to take into account. The husband's occupational pension stayed with him in the community. Part of the financial difficulty also for some spouses was that they had got used to income from social security benefits such as the attendance allowance while the cared-for person was looked after at home. A permanent admission to a care home meant the withdrawal of the attendance allowance from the household income.

Five family caregivers (two spouses and three adult children) reported that a private pension was being used towards the cost of care. The mean private pension was £51 and the range was from £10 to £110 per week. When a couple have savings a local authority can demand a contribution towards meeting the care costs. More than one in three of the spouses in the sample were either currently paying care costs from savings or had done so in the past. The sums involved were often large. Taking into account only current payment, the mean amount for those actually contributing was £383 per month with a range from £15 to £1,000. The total sums involved were relatively modest in relation to the actual costs of care, with the maximum that any spouse reported having paid so far estimated at £14,000. However, this was, of course, a snapshot picture taken at one moment in time and some of the spouses in the sample would inevitably end up paying far greater sums. Although a couple with joint savings are entitled to divide them into two unequal parts to avoid the spouse in a care home from being assessed as having half the couple's total savings, it is uncertain how often this right is realised and put into practice.

Topping up local authority payments

Local authorities make their own decisions about appropriate baseline fees for different levels of care (see Chapter 2). It will be easier for potential residents and their family caregivers to find care homes with fees at the level of local authority baselines in some areas than in others. In any one area there may be only a limited number of homes that have fees at the local authority baseline. As we have seen in the previous chapter, a significant principle in the new legislation is that individuals should have the freedom to exercise a choice of care home. A person may enter a home that has a fee higher than an authority's baseline fee under a local authority contract providing a third party agrees to top up the payment and the local authority agrees that the care in the home meets an individual's assessed needs. A third party might be a charity or a relative. If that third person is also liable to support the client (i.e. is a spouse or a parent) topping up must come after that liability is taken into account (Dimond, 1997, p. 549). The person who is resident can top up the local authority payment to the care home out of moneys which are disregarded for the purpose of income support.

Topping up income support to meet the actual fees was extremely common under the old system of state funding in place before April 1993. A recent Joseph Rowntree Foundation funded study shows that only about half the residents in receipt of preserved rights funding have their fees covered (Laing, 1998). Although topping up is less common under the post-1993 system, 14% of elderly local authority-funded residents are supplemented by a third party top up.

Several family caregivers in the present study reported that the amount paid by a local authority to the care home looking after the cared-for person was being topped up. The sources for these topping up payments varied. In some cases a charity met the difference between care home charges and local authority payments. One of the wives, for example, described her husband as working for a charity which ran several nursing homes all his working life. When he himself needed admission to a care home, the charity accepted the local authority baseline fee even though it was considerably lower than normal charges. Churches may sometimes step in to help, particularly if a placement is in a care home run by the appropriate denomination. One of the husbands described his wife developing pre-senile dementia and needing nursing home care. At this point in his life his business had collapsed and he was declared bankrupt. A nursing home specialising in caring for people with dementia and run by a religious organisation cost considerably more than the local authority was prepared to pay and his local church agreed to meet the fee difference.

Sons and daughters may feel that they have to top up local authority payments. Although this may not cause problems, it is an open-ended commitment as a parent may live for years and there is nothing to stop care homes raising their fees as often as they like. One of the daughters interviewed had entered into an agreement to top up which became difficult to maintain. She and her brother had decided on a suitable home after visiting 20 homes because it seemed to offer a high quality of care. Feeling that their father needed a stimulating environment the other homes had been rejected because residents were left to sit doing nothing or because of a pervasive smell of urine. The daughter enthused about the care home:

> *Nowhere smells. If there was a problem with any smell, they see to it, they change a carpet, or they make sure everyone changes their clothes, and they look proper. They've got the most wonderful beautiful garden with beautiful rose bushes and big lawns where they can sit out, and in the summertime on a Sunday they usually do gala parties and things like that for them. Not often, but quite a few times. If there's a birthday they make a big thing about it. They're always taking pictures, they go on the river, they go to the theatre, they go to lots of places.*

Both the brother and sister had signed an agreement with the local authority to meet the difference between the fee charged and the amount the local authority was prepared to pay. Their understanding was that if they failed to pay the top up their father would be moved to a cheaper care home. In the two years since the placement not only had the care home fees increased several times, the daughter had also been made redundant. It had become increasingly difficult to keep paying the top ups and the daughter had been forced to take out loans to keep up the payments.

Meeting extra costs in the care home
The fees paid to a care home are unlikely to meet all the costs that a resident will have. If a resident receives income support, part of it will be retained by the resident or relative to meet personal expenses. A personal expenses allowance is intended to allow a degree of personal spending. Department of Health guidance on Charging for Residential Accommodation (CRAG) gives the following definition: 'the personal expenses allowance is intended to enable residents to have money to spend as they wish, for example, on stationery, personal toiletries, treats and small presents for friends and relatives. The resident will normally supply their own clothes' (Department of Health, 1994b, par. 5.001). The value of this personal expenses allowance is currently £14.45 per week (financial year April 1998/99). It has been argued that the amount is far too low. A recent Age Concern England publication, *Money to Spend as They Wish*, argues that a more realistic figure would be £37.80 which would provide a 'modest-but-adequate' or reasonable living standard (Parker, 1997).

The adequacy or otherwise of the personal expenses allowance is related to what the fee charged by the care home actually covers and what the resident concerned wants to purchase. Care homes in fact vary widely in what is included in the fees charged. A small study carried out by the author for Age Concern England in 16 residential and nursing homes reported considerable variation in what was included (Wright, 1993). Although chiropody was available free of charge in some homes, in others residents had to pay for it. Clothes, underwear and shoes generally had to be purchased by the individual resident concerned. In a few care homes, however, a care home manager had a budget to make such purchases. Alcoholic drinks were available free of charge two or three times a week in a few care homes, but in most care homes could not be purchased even by a resident prepared to pay extra.

Most family caregivers in the current study handled finances for the cared-for person and were well aware of extra costs. Virtually all reported that hairdressing had to be paid for. A few people had to pay extra for incontinence supplies and two people had to pay for physiotherapy. One wife was amazed that she had to pay extra for chiropody. When her husband had lived at home, chiropody had been free but in the nursing home she had to find the money to pay for a private chiropodist. All the family caregivers commented on the amount that had to be spent on clothing. Underwear and night-clothes often had to be replaced frequently because the vigorous washing process in the care home caused premature wear and tear. One of the daughters voiced a common complaint:

> *I think it's far too much. They've taken every penny she's got. She's got no decent clothes. That's one of the financial problems that we have – trying to keep up with a washing machine that all your jumpers – everything just goes in. I can understand why they do it – a lot of people have accidents because a lot of them are incontinent. To be sure they put everything on a very hot wash and unfortunately all the jumpers go in and it ruins them. Her vests and pants – there are holes in them within weeks.*

Dry cleaning bills were also a frequently mentioned expense, particularly for some of the men who were sometimes incontinent or spilt food or drink.

Many family caregivers purchased items such as favourite foods or made sure that they provided drinks, fruit juice and squash as well as alcoholic drinks. Several care homes organised formal outings and hired a coach to take residents out for the day. Such outings were an additional cost. A small number of the residents concerned had a telephone in their rooms and this involved the cost of the rental and phone calls.

Estimating irregular expenditure is obviously problematic and very approximate. Just under half the family caregivers interviewed, however, thought that the additional costs occurring in the care home were covered by the personal expenses allowance. Over half thought that this was not the case and that it had to be supplemented either out of the resident's savings or by a family caregiver.

Additional costs for the caregivers
Two out of three family caregivers reported that the cared-for person moving into a care home had given them some additional costs to meet. All of them had some cost involved in making the journey to the care home. Wife caregivers had the highest costs of all. None of those interviewed drove a car but they had to travel to care homes which were rarely on convenient public transport routes. Half of them visited either daily or as often as five times a week. None visited less than three times a week. Although friends, neighbours and relatives provided a few lifts, most had to pay the cost of taxis both to and from the care homes.

Losing a future inheritance
Because a resident's savings are taken into account daughters and sons will forfeit moneys that they might reasonably have expected to inherit when the cared-for person died. A few offspring admitted that they had not been disinherited because a parent's assets had not been disclosed. One of the daughters, for example, had borrowed money from her mother to build an extension. That money had been repaid but into a specific bank account in the daughter's name to avoid it being taken by the local authority. The daughter insisted that, with the agreement of her siblings, she was doing the sensible thing and holding the money in trust. Not surprisingly as most of them administered a parent's moneys, the daughters and sons were only too conscious of the sums involved. Over half reported that there were parental savings that were either currently being used or had been used in the past until reduced to the limits. When there had been savings to be used, the mean total used since the parent's admission to a care home was £15,596 and the maximum amount so far used was £44,484. A third of daughters and sons reported that a parent had previously been an owner occupier and in most cases the houses involved had either been sold already or were in the process of being sold. Their response to being disinherited will be discussed in Chapter 6.

In conclusion

Although most spouse caregivers had been caring for people more dependent than those where daughters or sons were involved, they were less likely to have had support from services from outside the home whether statutory or private. When the cared-for person had moved into a care home, family caregivers made some savings on costs. Areas of savings included direct costs on services or goods and savings on time. Spouses who after all shared a household with the cared-for person were far more likely than daughters or sons to have personally had to meet direct costs such as payment for day care or services or household bills. Because of the high dependency of many of those being looked after, most spouse caregivers were more likely than daughters or sons to spend large amounts of time on caregiving. Nevertheless some of the daughters living in a different household from the parent did have to spend large amounts of time each day providing care. Several daughters had given up paid employment to meet the cared-for person's needs.

When asked what they had known about the current system of paying for care in a residential or nursing home before the point of the cared-for person needing admission, many family caregivers said they had been under the impression that the NHS met the costs. Some family caregivers reported that they only began to understand fundamental aspects of the current system such as taking a resident's savings into account months after the cared-for person's admission. Given the complexities and the inequities of the current system for spouses, it is not surprising that many of them remained confused. There can be no doubt that spouses in different local authority areas and in contact with different individual social workers in those areas were experiencing different systems of penalties for their partners being admitted to a care home. Local authority treatment of property rights can have far-reaching effects on the spouses remaining in the community. If some local authorities claim half the capital difference if the spouse remaining in the community wishes to move house, this may have enormous repercussions in its impact on the quality of that person's life.

Many family caregivers had to meet some or all of the costs of long-term care. Several were involved in topping up the amount paid by the local authority to secure the type of care home wanted. There were also extra costs such as providing clothes, food and drink. Although about half the family caregivers thought that the personal expenses allowance covered these extra costs, half thought that it was not adequate. Many of the spouses had additional travel costs. None of the wives, for example, drove a car and usually had to hire taxis to reach the care homes which were rarely situated on convenient public transport routes. As most visited several times a week, travel costs could be quite formidable. Spouses were financially affected by joint savings being taken into account. The rules regarding capital limits appear to be widely misunderstood by local authority employees and family caregivers. Half the daughters and sons interviewed had been effectively disinherited and had seen a parent's savings and capital disappear in meeting care costs. Several caregivers administrating the cared for person's savings had continued to pay out each month even though they had fallen well below the statutory limits.

Role of caregivers in the care home

Introduction

A wide literature from both sides of the Atlantic indicates that many family caregivers suffer both psychological and physical stress as a result of providing support and care in a domestic setting (Wright, 1986; Qureshi and Walker, 1989; Twigg *et al.*, 1990; Nolan *et al.*, 1996). Such stress may be extreme if the person being cared for suffers from dementia (Levin *et al.*, 1989). If the cared-for person enters a residential or nursing care home, many elements of the situation inevitably change. Staff in the care home now take a central role in the care process. But what role does a family caregiver now have or want to have when a cared-for person lives permanently in a care home? A research objective was to look at the extent to which family caregivers continued, or wished to continue, caregiving activities in the care home.

This chapter begins by considering existing good practice guidance in respect of the role of family caregivers when a cared-for person enters a care home. Visiting patterns of family caregivers in the sample are then described. The chapter then focuses on family caregivers' perceptions of their relationship with the cared-for person in the institutional setting and concludes by looking at the role family caregivers take in the care home.

Good practice guidance

Given the significance of family members to older people, it is rather surprising that good practice guidance has relatively little to say about how staff should behave towards relatives or what role relatives could, or should, take when an older person becomes resident in a care home. The Wagner report, *A Positive Choice*, gave relatives only a cursory mention: 'links should be maintained with friends and relatives who should be able to give support and practical care to residents if the latter so wish' (Wagner, 1988, p. 63). A National Institute for Social Work

(NISW) publication which followed the Wagner report and looked at the implications of research for improving the quality of life in residential care saw involving relatives as part of creating a more stimulating environment:

> *Relatives who continue to visit and take an active interest should be encouraged to participate in the residents' continuing care. This also requires changes of attitude and role of care assistants who have to enable this to happen.* (National Institute for Social Work, 1988, p. 27)

A recently published code of practice for residential and nursing home care by the Centre for Policy on Ageing (CPA), *A Better Home Life: A Code of Practice for Residential and Nursing Homes,* offers more specific but still rather circumspect advice:

> *Relatives and friends have an important role to play within homes. They should be encouraged to participate in the daily life of the home as long as the resident wants them to. This might involve sharing meals, doing shopping, washing hair, reading and other social activities. Some homes may wish to draw up agreements or contracts with relatives and friends, setting out what each party might be expected to do or provide. Having relatives actively involved in the home is likely to act as a check on possible abusive behaviour by staff.* (Centre for Policy on Ageing, 1996, par. 4.9.2)

Although the Social Services Inspectorate *Guidance on Standards for Residential Homes for Elderly People* has little to say about an appropriate role for relatives, it commented that a 'good' home would ensure that residents can meet people, have conversations, make or receive telephone calls, correspond and receive visitors, without being overlooked or overheard and without having to account to anyone for their actions (Department of Health\SSI, 1990, p. 19).

Preservation of relationships with relatives, friends, GPs, church and clubs was also described in this guidance as a way of a resident maintaining identity and individuality (Department of Health\SSI, 1990, p. 26).

Although both the Wagner report and the SSI report, *Homes are for Living in*, make it clear that residents themselves should handle their own finances as far as possible (Wagner, 1988, par. 4.16; Department of Health\SSI, 1989, p. 12, principle 3), recent CPA guidance designated a specific role to relatives in handling a resident's money because this was an area open to abuse by care staff:

> *Relatives should handle social security benefits, other finances and fee payment if nominated by the resident.* (Centre for Policy on Ageing, 1996, par. 6.91)

Contact with the cared-for person

UK studies of residential care in both the public and independent sectors confirm that most residents receive regular visits from both family members and friends (Weaver *et al.*, 1985; Willcocks *et al.*, 1986; Neill *et al.*, 1988). Family caregivers in the current study were no exception and reported regularly visiting the cared-for person. American studies of nursing home care also indicate frequency of contact between residents and relatives (Smith and Bengston, 1979; Kahana *et al.*, 1985; Schwartz and Vogel, 1990). Differences were apparent in the current study between spouses and offspring in the frequency of visits. As in other studies, spouses were likely to visit frequently (Nolan and Grant, 1992) and half visited either daily or as often as five times per week. Few visited as little as once a week. In contrast more than half the daughters and sons visited weekly and just under half more frequently.

A visit may of course be any length of time from ten minutes to the whole day. Some spouses did report spending the whole day every day in the care home. One of the wives whose husband had suffered a major stroke, for example, aimed to arrive in the nursing home at 10.00 a.m. and usually remained there until 8.00 p.m. when her son or grandson came to take her home. Even longer was spent by one of the husbands who aimed to arrive at his wife's nursing home at about 8.30 a.m. After helping his wife with dressing and eating breakfast he then usually spent the whole day with her. To his annoyance the matron insisted that he had to go home by 9.00 p.m.

The venue
When a person lives in an institution, whether it be a prison, boarding school or care home, the venue for a relative or friend's visit becomes all-important. Privacy is likely to encourage a relationship but lack of privacy is likely to be intimidating to both resident and visitor. In a nursing or residential care home the choice of venue is usually limited. It may be possible to take the cared-for person out to a public place like a pub or a restaurant or to the privacy of a family caregiver's own home. On the whole options within a care home will be restricted to a choice between a bedroom, a communal lounge or, weather and facilities permitting, a garden area. Other studies have commented on how rarely residents actually go out of care homes. A study of the physical and social influences on 100 people with senile dementia in residential care found that only 11% went out of the home at least once a month with relatives (Netten, 1993). Differences were evident in the current study between spouses and offspring in whether the cared-for person accompanied a family caregiver out of a care home. Although hardly any spouse caregivers had taken their partner out, many sons and daughters had taken a parent out at least occasionally by car for a meal or simply for a drive. Such differences between spouses and adult children arose from their different situations. Generally spouses were more likely than daughters or sons to have sustained looking after someone with very high dependency in the community. Many of those looked after by spouses had severe dementia by the time they had entered a care home. It can be very difficult to take a dementia sufferer for an outing as one of the husband's experiences illustrates. He ruefully described his efforts to take his wife out for a drive:

She never goes out. I tried to get her into the car to go out for a little ride when we had some lovely weather last year. But she got as far as the door of the car and then I said, 'Well, sit down'. And she'd sit on the pavement! I said, 'You get in and you put your bottom in first'. She got there, I got that part in. But she wouldn't pick her legs up to go in. The matron came out and said, 'I'll help her', and she wanted to pick her legs up, and my wife hit out at her. So then we decided the best thing was to go back in the home.

Wife caregivers had their own problems in organising outings. Although virtually all the sons, daughters and husbands had cars or access to cars, this was not the case for these women. None of the wives interviewed had a car and all relied on public transport or a taxi to visit their husbands. Their own mobility had been severely curtailed when their husbands had become dependent and unable to drive a car. Without a car it would have been very difficult for them to physically take their husbands out of the care home. Even without problems of this kind, caregivers were often worried about causing a dementia sufferer distress by taking her or him back home. It was commonly argued that taking any kind of trip would only increase the cared-for person's confusion.

I've never had him home for the reason that I just wonder whether he even remembers home. When they get into a rut and a routine, to take them out of that I think personally is unfair, because it disturbs a lot of memories that perhaps might upset him and distress him. And they've said, 'You can have him home if you want, but he's quite happy here, why disturb him'. So that's why. (Wife)

A further factor inhibiting family caregivers from organising outings was the obvious institutionalisation of a cared-for person. When leaving the care home caused such distress there seemed little value in it:

And as I say she gets insecure when she's out. She always wants to get back to The Hollies. 'Is it time yet? We've been out a long time now. Let's go now.' All that. So it's not really worth it and she gets all agitated if you've got to put her coat on. It's not worth disrupting her, you know. (Daughter)

Inevitably then most contact between a family caregiver and a cared-for person took place at the care home. Privacy was not feasible in most care homes because bedrooms were not private bed sitting rooms. They were either too small to accommodate a visitor in any comfort or were shared. In any case the residents concerned were not the age group to consider a bedroom an appropriate place to meet visitors. Although in some care homes it was possible to find a quiet corner in a corridor or even a special visitors' lounge, many visits took place in a public place, the communal lounge. The title of a well-known study of local authority home, *Private Lives in Public Places*, is unfortunately still a very apt description of life in a care home (Willcocks *et al.*, 1987). Meeting in a public place, however, offered welcome distractions to some, particularly if the resident concerned had little to communicate. One of the wives relished her daily visits to the care home:

> *I meet my husband in the lounge. It's lovely because you get to know everybody anyway. And if he goes to sleep I just help out which I had a card to thank me for and a chocolate orange!*

On the other hand, meeting in a communal lounge could cause some family caregivers considerable distress. A wife in her eighties felt that her relationship with her husband had been virtually destroyed by always meeting him in public. No seat was ever available, or proffered, near her husband and other residents were reluctant to move from their established chairs. As she always had to sit some distance away from her husband the only way to overcome his partial deafness was to shout:

> *George, my husband, is always telling us not to shout, because he says they're all listening. He's got that idea that they're all listening to one another and eavesdropping and tale-telling and things like that. He gets that idea, and says, 'Don't talk so loud.'*

Lack of privacy when a cared-for person had become confused could be particularly distressing. As her mother had to share a bedroom, one of the daughters could only meet her mother in the communal lounge. She felt humiliated by the amusement her mother's conversation generated amongst other residents and their visitors:

> *Being deaf, I do think they ought to have a separate room where parents can have visitors. Much more personal. And I kind of feel I'm entertaining the whole lounge. Yes I do feel the past couple of times I was in there, she was really wandering. I took my daughter and one of the grandsons in and she was saying some stupid things and she had the whole of the rest of the lounge in fits of laughter.*

Visiting a parent or a husband or wife with advanced dementia is likely to be a painful experience whatever the venue. Several family caregivers reported no longer being recognised. One of the sons who visited each week had got used to the lack of recognition:

The difficulty is that my mother usually does not recognise me. I have got used to it and I just take a book and sit next to her reading. Usually she says, 'Who are you?', but sometimes she will recognise me towards the end.

Meals
Meals in care homes are major events. An account of what it is like to work in residential homes described meal-times as punctuating the general inactivity with bursts of movement, an important feature of daily routine and one of the most central occasions for talking to others (Brearley, 1990). When a family caregiver and a resident share a meal whether in the care home or outside it is a significant social activity for both of them. As a study of the impact of bereavement on whether, and in what way, food behaviour changed as a result of losing a partner concluded: 'meal-taking provides an opportunity for people to meet, talk, share problems and celebrate successes' (Howarth, 1993, p. 77). The recently published code of good practice for residential and nursing home care, quoted earlier, acknowledged that sharing meals is one way for friends and relatives to share in the daily life of a care home (Centre for Policy on Ageing, 1996, par. 4.92). A recent Counsel and Care publication on good practice around food and meal-times in care homes for older people recommended that homes should encourage residents to invite visitors to meals, especially in situations where a visitor comes regularly or for long periods, or is available to help the resident eat and drink (Chester and Davies, 1996). Few family caregivers reported regularly having a proper meal at the care home. Apart from the few spouses who sat with and helped to care for their partners all day, several spouses but only two of the daughters regularly shared a meal at least weekly with the cared-for person in the care home. One of the wives concerned was very assertive often bringing a take-away to share with her husband. She regularly took a curry to the home, shut her husband's bedroom door and they pretended to be in their own home at least for a short time.

From care staff's perspective there are obvious practical difficulties in encouraging relatives to stay for meals. Kitchen staff need to know how many people they are preparing meals for. Unless relatives gave notice that they would like to dine at the care home, it would be difficult to know how much food to prepare. It was noticeable that only one respondent, a daughter, reported that she could spontaneously decide to stay for a meal at any time. In addition meal-times are a very busy time for care staff. Not only do many residents have to be helped to use the toilet before meals and assisted to the table; in some cases, supervision was needed for a meal to be successfully eaten. It is a point of the day when the level of activity would make it difficult for staff to give attention to visitors. Excluding visitors can be seen as part of the process of institutionalisation. Staff may feel that if relatives are present their own control of a significant aspect of the day's proceedings could be under threat. In reality many family caregivers may be reluctant to stay at meal-times when residents are dementia sufferers. A common aspect of this disease at the later stages is an absence of conventional table manners. Some of the family caregivers described cared-for people forgetting how to use a knife and fork or being confused about the function of plates. One of the wives described her distress at seeing her husband finish what was on his plate and then start scraping the tablecloth with gusto. Another wife found it terrible that her husband no longer knew how to put food in his mouth and poured food down his clothes. Both wives ensured that they were not present at meal-times.

Staff were obviously in a powerful position to encourage or discourage relatives from taking a meal in a care home. One of the sons reported that he had paid for and eaten a sandwich with his mother while she ate her Sunday lunch for several weeks. This practice was stopped at the request of the staff:

> But I had to stop doing that because the staff were willing to do a sandwich (which I paid for) but said that the other residents were upset at the idea that I should see people with dementia eating food.

Some family caregivers had been invited to participate in a meal with the cared-for person on a special occasion only. Spouses were more likely than sons or daughters to have been invited in this way. Four different types of special circumstances were mentioned. One was as part of the admission process to the care home.

Only the first time I went in, when I took him in, that day. It was just teatime. So she said, 'Would you like to stay to tea with him? Settle him down a bit.' So I did stay to tea that time, but I haven't stayed since. (Wife)

No. We did when she first went round when they wanted to assess her and she went to have a look. They gave her a meal and I had a meal there. But I've never been offered one since. (Husband)

Inevitably a meal in such circumstances takes on symbolic significance. A last shared meal was taken at the threshold of the institution. One partner then entered the institution and the other returned home.

A second type of occasion for a meal being offered was Christmas. Several spouses had had Christmas dinner with their partners in the care home. Others would have liked the opportunity but had never been invited:

I wouldn't mind Christmas time but they've never suggested it – you see they haven't got many staff. (Wife)

The third type of occasion was special celebrations for birthdays or anniversaries. One of the wives whose husband had had a stroke was appreciative of the kindness staff showed:

It was our wedding anniversary and they put on a special meal for us in a special room – just the two of us and they provided it all. It was all done very nicely.

A special occasion for the care home such as an annual garden party or an anniversary of the home being founded was the fourth type of occasion for a meal being shared with the cared-for person in the care home.

Although none of the spouses managed to take the cared-for person out for a meal or a sociable drink in a pub or a restaurant, several daughters and sons took a parent out occasionally or had done so in the past. On a really special occasion staff sometimes assisted in a meal being taken outside the care home. One of the wives described her delight when two members of staff, one to drive the car and the other to assist her husband, gave up their evening to take her and her husband out on her birthday for a Chinese meal. Despite relatively few family caregivers taking proper meals in the care homes, most had been offered, and accepted, tea and biscuits during their visits.

Relationship between family caregiver and cared-for person

Maintaining a cared-for person in her or his own home in the community is generally of high importance to family caregivers (Nolan *et al.*, 1996). This is often accomplished, however, at the cost of considerable caregiver stress, particularly if the cared-for person suffers from dementia. In these circumstances family caregivers may reach the point of being unable to cope either physically or emotionally with the cared-for person's need for continual support. One of the most stressful later life events is generally acknowledged to be the admission of the cared-for person to long-term institutional care. Such a move is likely to be traumatic both for caregiver and for the cared-for person (see Chapter 3). As neither caregiver nor cared-for person tends to be knowledgeable about care homes, part of the trauma is a fear of the unknown. Inevitably a cared-for person entering long-term care is likely to have repercussions for family relationships. Whether a spouse or offspring, a family caregiver is likely to feel a mixture of strong emotions such as guilt, relief, and worry about the future. A newly admitted resident is also likely to experience a mixture of emotions such as anger, bewilderment, apprehension, guilt and feelings of rejection.

Relationship between parent and offspring
Differences were apparent between adult children and spouses in respect of reported relationships with the cared-for person after the admission to a care home. The relationships described by daughters and sons tended to fall into one of three broad categories:

* a close relationship both before and after admission

* a poor relationship both before and after admission

* an improved relationship following admission.

One in three daughters and sons described their relationship with a parent as close both before and after the admission to a care home. Approximately the same proportion thought the relationship had definitely been poor and continued to be so. But the remaining third thought the relationship with a parent had positively been improved by the move. Relationships had been strained previously by the problems of sustaining the parent in some kind of normal existence in the community. Simple everyday personal care activities such as eating a meal or using the toilet could be a source of tension. When the parent entered the care home, the daughter or son no longer felt a responsibility to constantly check up on whether meals had been eaten or the toilet used.

I felt I was just nagging her – I never went and just had a pleasant visit – it was all pressure, pressure, pressure, because I was so desperate for her not to give up her home unless there was obviously absolutely no choice. (Daughter)

When an assistant in the care home took responsibility for supervising personal care activities, some caregivers found the space to re-establish a relationship:

Really it has improved because we don't now have to ask her to do anything controversial. So when I go in to talk to my mother I can take her for a walk in the gardens and talk about the butterflies and the fish in the pond and everything like that. Whereas before it was all very controversial because we were saying, 'Come on Mum and eat your meal. We've got to take you to the toilet.' All that sort of thing. (Son)

Other research has confirmed the strengthening of family ties in similar circumstances. An American study using open-ended interviews with 100 elderly parents admitted to a care home and their middle-aged children focused on information about pre-admission contact and events leading to institutionalisation (Smith and Bengston, 1979). A third of the sample of both parents and their middle-aged children reported renewed closeness and strengthening of family ties following the admission to institutional care.

Relationship between spouses

In contrast none of the spouses living in the community thought there had been any improvement in their relationship with their partners following the latter's admission to a care home. Although a few thought their relationship had remained good despite a husband or wife's admission, most did not. They either described a relationship that had been poor before the admission and remained poor afterwards or that had deteriorated on admission. Descriptions of the cared-for person's resentment were common. One of the husbands who had been unable to cope with his wife's dementia at home when she became doubly incontinent could hardly bear to visit because of her anger:

She knows me when I go in. She knows I've come to see her, and the expression that comes back is, 'What the hell do you want?' You know, it's that sort of reaction I get.

Another husband, continually under attack when he visited, commented ruefully:

Sometimes she calls me a stinker or a bitch. She might call me a dog but a bitch!

When as many as one in three offspring reported an improvement in their relationship with the cared-for person after an admission to a care home, it is perhaps surprising that this occurred with none of the spouses. The resentment expressed by many of those who had previously been cared for by spouses was fuelled by the different expectations in our society in respect of obligations to provide support. In fact those who had previously been looked after by a spouse at home had generally needed more help with self-care than those supported by daughters or sons (see Chapter 3). A spouse had been more likely to personally provide care than a daughter or son. Paid community support staff were more likely to give personal care when offspring were caregivers. Less is expected of adult children than is expected of spouses. As a study of caring relationships in Sheffield demonstrated, people allocate responsibility for providing care to an older person needing support according to a hierarchy of obligations; a spouse has the strongest obligation followed by a daughter then a daughter-in-law then a son and then a son-in-law (Qureshi and Simons, 1987). Older parents still have a feeling of obligation towards their middle-aged children. 'A significant element of imbalance exists in the character of the commitment each side feels within the relationship: parents' commitment to the child is likely to be stronger than the latter's commitment to them' (Allan, 1988, p. 252). Although an older parent may be reluctant to enter a care home, guilt at causing problems to a middle-aged child may mitigate any feelings of resentment.

Resentment is more likely to be expressed towards a spouse caregiver because of the belief that a husband or wife should continue to provide support and care whatever the odds. Finch (1995) suggests that spouse responsibilities conform more closely to a model of fixed obligations than do adult child responsibilities. Marriage is viewed differently from other family relationships. 'All this would suggest that caring for one's spouse may well be viewed as an intrinsic part of being married, not dependent upon the particular relationship which any individual has with a husband or wife' (Finch, 1995, p. 54). There are indications that expectations of a spouse are even higher in the UK than in many other countries. Evidence from an International Social Survey programme indicated that, by comparison with some other European countries, British respondents tended to say that their spouse is the first person to whom they would turn for help when ill (Finch, 1995).

On the whole spouses were more likely than daughters or sons to express guilt at the cared-for person being in a care home and to report the cared-for person wanting to return home.

> *Oh she keeps on wanting to come out with me, saying, 'Are you going to take me out now? Are we going out?' They all do. That's one thing they've all got in common – they all want to go home.* (Husband)

> *Then when I'm leaving, I don't know whether she thinks I've come to take her away, that she's going to come with me … Very confusing. I hate it.* (Husband)

One of the wives had to help her husband move to a different care home, when a placement failed because of his aggressive behaviour:

I went there with this huge bag that we used to use for our holidays to bring his clothes away. He saw me at the end of this long corridor and he hugged me and hugged me as if he'd never hugged me before. He thought he was coming home you see.

A contributory factor in wanting or expecting to return home is that a resident with a spouse living at home still has a home in the community. Parents who had been widowed and then gone into a care home would rarely be in that position. If the previous home had been rented the tenancy would have been given up, and if it had been owned, it would have been sold to meet the costs of care.

Relationships with care staff

In a dependency situation in the community a family caregiver occupies an ambiguous role in relation to service providers. They exist off-centre to service provision. The relationship between the two is uncertain and ill-defined. Carers are not clients or patients, and they are rarely the direct focus of an intervention; and yet at the same time they are clearly part of the complexities of care that service providers have to recognise (Twigg and Atkin, 1994, p. 11). The ambiguity is not resolved if a cared-for person enters long-term care. With the exception of people who have suffered a stroke and then become dependent, the period before admission is likely to have been dominated by a caregiver's need to give the cared-for person increasing amounts of attention and support. Although some of the good practice guidance referred to earlier in the chapter talks of the importance of relatives, the role they can actually play depends on many interrelated factors. Most family caregivers had little or no previous experience of care homes. Their role in that new setting had to be established in negotiation with the care home manager, individual care staff and the cared-for person.

Managers and care staff might well have different perspectives from each other about an appropriate family caregiver role. Most care assistants are part-time and have had no social work training. Many managers of care homes themselves are not professionally trained. The Howe report on the quality of residential care, written for the Local Government Management Board, referred to the relatively poor image and status of residential care both in the eyes of the public and of other professional groups (Howe, 1992). Care staff's low morale was a key theme in the evidence to the Wagner review of residential care (Wagner, 1988). Lack of training and low pay were identified in the report as key factors in this low morale. Care staff have their own work problems. Care assistants are usually on manual pay grades. Staff shortages are common in care homes because other local jobs are likely to be available at higher rates of pay. If there is a low staff to resident ratio, care assistants are under considerable pressure. When residents are dementia sufferers, care assistants may find themselves in a situation for which they have had no training or relevant previous experience. Good practice guidance on the potential role of relatives in a care home is unlikely to be familiar unless it has featured in discussions or in-house training within the care home. Care assistants were in a particularly powerful position. Not only were family caregivers new to care home procedures and practices, they were also anxious not to upset staff and thereby jeopardise the well-being of the cared-for person. Studies of staff in care homes on both sides of the Atlantic show an enormous gap between staff who have been professionally trained and those who have not in their approach to care. A study of five nursing homes in the UK, for example, found that, although matrons and qualified staff talked about social care, nursing assistants who had not been trained placed little value on the social aspects of care (Bartlett, 1993) and reported being too busy to talk to residents. A similar study of American nursing homes concluded that, although matrons and registered nurses believed the psycho-social needs of residents to be important, untrained nursing assistants revealed little awareness of such aspects of care (Kane and Kane, 1987).

Family caregivers' relationships with care staff are likely to be affected by the guilt inevitably accompanying the cared-for person's admission to care. A decision about the appropriateness of a care home is generally taken in response to a crisis and is often precipitated by stress. Although research shows that the level of caregiver stress is reduced by the admission of the cared-for person to long-term institutional care (Levin *et al.*, 1989, 1994), a considerable body of research also indicates that the mental health of family caregivers remains adversely affected (Brody *et al.*, 1990; Ritchie and Ledesert, 1992; Rosenthal *et al.*, 1993). One study of the phases of transition of a dementing older person entering institutional care suggested that, although admission brought relief from the primary effects of caregiving (e.g. feelings of overload and tension) and improved well-being, other indicators of stress remained unchanged (Zarit and Whitlach, 1992). Overall, the results of this study suggest that the careers of caregivers do not stop at the institution's door but continue in an altered and still stressful way. Caregivers do not give up their role, they shift their responsibilities (Zarit and Whitlack, p. 672).

Research in a hospital setting indicated that staff and relatives may hold divergent views about the nature and extent of contact between them. A study of a day hospital resource to support relatives, for example, showed that staff thought they gave relatives extensive support by providing frequent contact between home and hospital, by acting as a source of advice on patient management and care, and providing emotional support and therapy (Smith and Cantley, 1985). For their part, however, relatives were unlikely to hold this view of staff behaviour. Few incidents were mentioned of staff giving information about an older person's illness or advice on how to cope.

Family caregivers' satisfaction with care home
Despite reservations about some aspects of care or some members of staff, it was striking how positive most family caregivers were about the care home as a whole. Spouses were particularly likely to express satisfaction. One husband's sentiment was echoed by many:

Oh I'm very satisfied with the home, you couldn't have a nicer home, as far as I know, because I haven't been in all that lot.

Studies on both sides of the Atlantic have also commented on the high level of positive satisfaction with care homes expressed by family caregivers (Smith and Bengston, 1979; Gladstone, 1995; Grau *et al.*, 1995). A recent survey carried out by the Alzheimer's Disease Society (1997) in the UK, for example, of relatives' views of residential and nursing care homes reported that as many as 85% were happy with the care provided. Similarly Scottish case studies of six residential homes in all sectors found that 72% of relatives had no criticism to make; any fault-finding tended to focus on aspects of the buildings (Bland *et al.*, 1992). Although so many studies indicate such a high level of relatives' satisfaction, it cannot be concluded that the care homes concerned were necessarily of high quality. Most family caregivers interviewed in the current study admitted having little idea about care homes until a place had to be found for the cared-for person, often at a crisis point (see Chapter 3). Although few caregivers had previously been to a care home, many had experienced the cared-for person being in hospital. Care homes are likely to compare favourably to hospitals. Designed as transitory places for the sick, hospitals consist of wards with relatively little privacy and rarely include sitting or dining rooms. In contrast most care homes with bedrooms separate from lounges and dining rooms offer a better quality of life. A factor influencing whether family caregivers expressed satisfaction with the care home was their age. Spouses were generally in their seventies and eighties. Half the daughters were aged 60 or more. Age, as Coleman (1990) pointed out, is related to expressed satisfaction. Older people display much higher rates of satisfaction with all aspects of their lives except health than younger generations.

A family caregiver's role
Family caregivers described their role in the care home in some detail. A hierarchy of helping behaviour was in evidence:

1	checking the quality of care

2	companionship

3	handling finances

4	shopping

5	transportation

6	doing laundry

7	assisting the cared-for person with personal care such as:
  - eating a meal
  - taking a bath

- using the toilet
- dressing.

Checking the quality of care
Family caregivers no longer took direct and total daily responsibility for hands-on care. Their involvement with the cared-for person was now of a different kind. A prime concern now was to ensure that the cared-for person's needs were being met. Although the majority of caregivers expressed satisfaction with the care home as a whole, as many as half found fault with some aspect of the care. Shortcomings were often attributed to the pressure exerted on care assistants by staff shortages and high rates of staff turnover.

Well it's good and bad. They're very good, very good. Sometimes they forget his tablets and to wash and shave him. But if they haven't got the staff on what can you do about it? (Wife)

They're badly understaffed. But on the whole they do the best they can with the staff they've got. (Daughter)

I have to keep my eye on things to make sure they keep up the standard of care, simply because there's so many demands on them. (Wife concerned that nursing staff did not turn husband frequently enough to prevent pressure sores)

Staff shortages have been identified as an issue in studies of both nursing and residential care homes (Bartlett, 1993; Wright, 1995; Alzheimer's Disease Society, 1997). A report examining issues of privacy in residential and nursing care homes commented that a heavy workload for staff combined with the pressures of communal life resulted in the daily life of the home often being characterised by routines, rules and regulation (Counsel and Care, 1991). One of the daughters in the current study observed the impact of hard routine work on staff behaviour:

They are overworked which means that the carers have to do the cleaning and they do the food. You name it, they do it. And I think they work very hard, but because they work so hard doing what they do, perhaps the more finite things are sometimes missed. So I think that there's room for improvement.

Four aspects of care came in for particular criticism: inadequate stimulation, poor standard of cleanliness, lack of respect for the dignity of the cared-for person and the overuse of drugs.

Inadequate stimulation. Lack of stimulation was an issue identified by several family caregivers. An area of particular concern was the failure of care assistants to initiate conversation with residents. One of the sons whose mother had advanced dementia felt that staff virtually ignored his mother and he was anxious about the lack of interaction:

I am not satisfied at all. I would like one of them to just sit and talk to her. They do not. All they do is say, 'Would you like a cup of tea, dear?', in a very loud voice. Nothing else is ever said. (Son)

Care homes can seem to be devoid of activity. Some caregivers were surprised by how little was happening in the care home:

The only thing, I wish they'd have a little bit more, perhaps going on. Sometimes you see where these homes, perhaps people come in and have a sing-song or something. (Daughter)

An absence of care home staff involvement in social care has been commented on in numerous studies which include resident and staff interaction (Willcocks *et al.*, 1987; Bartlett, 1993).

Poor standard of cleanliness. A lack of cleanliness worried several caregivers. Sometimes the issue was an incontinent person not being bathed frequently enough. One of the wives found herself continually checking with her husband who had to use incontinence pads how frequently staff bathed him. Although an answer only once every eight days seemed quite inadequate she felt unable to take up the issue because of a shortage of staff. An absence of hand washing worried some caregivers:

I think there are little things like her fingernails are always really filthy. Unfortunately she does see to her own toilet – you know when they go to the toilet they clean themselves. Her fingernails are just caked. I see her and I feel like getting a nail brush to her fingernails and I take her into the ladies. (Daughter)

Lack of respect for a resident's dignity. Maintaining the dignity of the cared-for person was all-important. Caregivers checked for clothes being neat, clean and smart, and for appearances being maintained:

Well yes. I expect he's got his oldest clothes on. I shall have to bring them home – that's the answer there. They were all right when he went there but he's been there 12 months and they keep washing them. That's the point. (Wife)

I turned up and my mum was wearing a pair of men's lace-up shoes, brown lace-up shoes and no tights. This was in the winter. I said, 'Why isn't my mum wearing any tights?' One girl said, 'We have no tights left'. And the other one said, 'Oh she's had a little accident'. So I said, 'Would you find another pair of tights please?' (Daughter)

So, if his hair is getting long I do mention it to them. I said, 'It's about time he had his hair done, and when is the hairdresser coming?' So they said, 'Oh he's due at certain times'. So I said, 'Oh well would you mind having it done, because he used to hate his hair getting long'. (Wife)

Overuse of drugs. Some family caregivers worried about the use of drugs in the care home. One daughter was upset because she felt her mother was being drugged for the staff's convenience:

And he said, 'She's quite quiet today'. So I said, 'Is she still being sedated?' because that's what they had to do because she was still lashing out. And he said, 'Yes. But it's okay because she sleeps very well at night'. Here she is – she's a living vegetable and they're still sedating her. It makes me so angry I can't tell you. (Daughter)

Another daughter felt she could never get a clear picture of what, if any, drugs were being used. Sometimes staff reported that her mother needed sleeping tablets but other times denied that such drugs would ever be used.

Companionship

As we have seen earlier in the chapter, family caregivers were regular visitors to the care home. Spouses visited very frequently: half of them at least five times per week. Visiting was a way of showing that the family caregiver still cared. Companionship was important to both parties. Visiting a dementia sufferer could be particularly painful to a family caregiver if there was a lack of recognition. One of the wives continued visiting three times a week despite her own mobility problems and her husband's failure to recognise her:

But now he's got to the stage that he's just accepting things. His brain isn't accepting me sometimes you see; he doesn't know who I am, until I start talking to him and that, and then one of the carers comes in and says, 'This is Frances, she's come to see you – your wife'. Then he looks up and he says, 'Oh, yes, all right'. And I can't converse with him at all.

Family caregivers sometimes had to accept being identified as a member of staff. One of the daughters insisted she had learnt to cope with her mother's failure to recognise her:

Sometimes she'll tug my sleeve and say, 'Miss'. She calls me 'miss'. She doesn't know it's me. Sometimes she says, 'Nurse, can you help me?' And I say, 'I'm not the nurse. I'm Anna.' And she says, 'Oh, are you? Sorry.' She forgets.

Handling finances

As described earlier in the chapter good practice guidance makes it clear that wherever possible residents should handle their own finances. If residents cannot, or do not want to, handle their own finances a relative or friend may do it for them. An Age Concern England publication, *Residents' Money: A Guide to Good Practice in Care Homes*, acknowledges that many people who live in a home may need some help to manage their money (Age Concern, 1996d, p. 12). Previous research carried out by the author looking at practices in handling residents' money, one for Anchor Housing Association in its Housing-with-Care schemes and the other for Age Concern England in a small sample of residential and nursing homes, concluded that few residents on income support handled their own fee payments or personal expenses allowances (Wright, 1993, 1994). Relatives and care staff handled finances for most residents. Central government guidance to local authorities is that, if there is no available close relative or friend willing to act and a local social services department is unable to recommend someone, then the person registered with the local authority under the Registered Homes Act 1984 for the home can be appointed but only as a last resort (Department of Health\SSI, 1989). Although in the current study family caregivers handled finances for four out of five people in care, care home managers were reported to take responsibility for the financial and fee payments of one in five residents, despite the obvious existence of concerned and involved relatives. About half of the family caregivers not handling a resident's finances were spouses and half, daughters. Although handling a resident's finances is a way in which most family caregivers get involved in the care process, it is not one that seems to generate positive feelings. Money from savings, pensions and income support has to be transferred from a resident's account to a local authority or direct to a home manager. The sums involved in paying contributions towards fees may seem intimidating to the family caregivers involved. Certainly the family caregivers not taking responsibility for finances seemed very relieved to have passed the responsibility to the care home.

Shopping, transportation and doing laundry
A small proportion of family caregivers, one in five, regularly went shopping and/or did laundry for the cared-for person. A similar proportion regularly took the cared-for person either out for leisure trips or provided transport to appointments at a hospital, the dentist or the optician. Although none of the wives of residents interviewed had cars, virtually all the other family caregivers did. It is a reflection of the high dependency of the residents involved that so few went out for a car drive. Few residents suffering dementia were taken out in a car. This appeared to be partly a response to some dementia sufferers' inability to understand the purpose of a car, and partly a fear of causing distress by reminding the dementia sufferer of the outside world and a past life.

Personal Care

Respondents were asked about any involvement in helping the cared-for person with personal care. Two spouses, one husband and one wife, did spend the whole day in the nursing home giving extensive personal care. Both helped their partners with eating, drinking and using the toilet, and by providing constant companionship. The majority of the cared-for people did need help with eating a meal. Although some caregivers regularly helped in this area there was almost no involvement in other types of personal care. Only two daughters, for example, helped a mother to take a bath and only one daughter ever helped her mother to use the toilet.

Did family caregivers want greater involvement in caregiving in the care homes?

As the guidance quoted earlier in the chapter makes clear, it is considered good practice to encourage relatives to participate in the daily life of the care home and take an active part in a resident's continuing care (National Institute for Social Work, 1988, p. 27; Wagner, 1988, p. 63; Centre for Policy on Ageing, 1996, par. 4.9.2). Most family caregivers lacked previous experience of care homes (see Chapter 3). When the cared-for person entered the care home, family caregivers had to undergo a learning process about their role in the new situation. Managers and care staff had a crucial role to play at an early stage in encouraging or discouraging caregivers' involvement in practical activities. Relationships between elderly residents and care staff in residential and nursing homes have been extensively documented. The literature indicates a juxtaposition. Residents highly value interaction with care staff over and above interaction with fellow residents and want staff to spend more time talking to them (Willcocks et al., 1987; Bartlett, 1993; Wright, 1995; Peace et al., 1997). Care assistants on the other hand do not appear to place a high value on the social aspects of their work. They tended to be preoccupied by physical care and to not like becoming too involved in social interaction with residents. When an appropriate role is perceived in this way, it may be very difficult for staff to involve family caregivers in caregiving.

The most significant roles family caregivers had in the care homes were checking on the quality of care, companionship and handling finances.

Shopping, transportation, doing laundry and assisting with personal care gave a relatively minor involvement for most of them. But did family caregivers want greater involvement in practical care for the cared-for person? Several daughters and sons made it very clear that they were relieved that their involvement in this sphere had come to an end. Helping a parent to take a bath or use the toilet broke established taboos. Help with using the toilet was an area which had previously upset several daughters. This comment was typical of several:

> *It's not good to be washing your mother's bottom and all that. It's not nice for her. I mean I can do all those things – I'm not at all squeamish. I can clear up. You say, 'That's how you used to clean me up'. She hated it. But at times it was absolutely necessary – I had to do it. There's nothing I want to do now!* (Daughter)

Spouses were far more likely than daughters and sons to have wanted to continue assisting the cared-for person in a practical way in the care home. Several spouses reported being strongly discouraged from practical involvement at an early stage. One wife, for example, expected to be able to continue cutting her husband's toe nails but was told in no uncertain terms that this was no longer her responsibility:

> *Once, at the beginning, he said, 'I wish somebody would cut my toe nails'. So me being used to it, and as we were sat out in the garden (they've a nice garden to sit out in), I said, 'I've got some scissors, shall I cut them while we're sat here?' So he said, 'Oh yes, because they've not cut my nails, and they're hurting a bit'. So of course I took his shoes off, and his socks, and clipped his nails for him, and I thought it was all right. And he was quite pleased about that, that I'd done this for him, so I put his shoes and socks back on and then I looked at his finger nails and they were a bit long so, he's always liked them short, so I clipped his finger nails as well. So we got back, but one of the carers, she had a word with me after, and she said, 'Would you mind not attending to your husband and doing things like that because we're supposed to do things like that, and to do them in the open is not acceptable'.*

An intervention by one of the husbands had similarly led to reproof. His wife who had severe dementia became very agitated at bedtime shortly after being admitted to a nursing home. Her husband helped her undress and go to bed, actions which had been undertaken routinely for the past five years in his own home. A care assistant took him to one side and explained that it was now a member of staff's job to get his wife ready for bed.

Some disabilities make eating a very slow process. Because of a fear that care staff would be too busy to spend enough time helping her husband eat a whole meal, one of the wives timed her visits so that she could give the necessary help. Although the manager was encouraging, care assistants made adverse comments when she collected the food from a trolley. Such conflict was a source of great worry to her in case the care assistants took out their annoyance on her husband. A recent study in Anchor care homes also reported that care staff were less positive than managers towards relatives (Oldman *et al.*, 1998). Other research confirms that spouses are more likely than other types of family caregivers to want to continue giving care in an institutional setting. A study of French family caregivers of institutionalised dementia sufferers, for example, indicated that spouses were twice as likely as adult children to express a desire to continue giving daily practical care (Ritchie and Ledesert, 1992). Extensive research in American nursing homes indicates that the extent to which a family is encouraged to participate in care for a resident significantly influences the adjustment of family members and residents' own adjustment to living in an institutional setting (Smith and Bengston, 1979; Buckwalter and Hall, 1987; Pratt *et al.*, 1987).

Care staff as key workers
A development designed to encourage better communication and interaction between residents and care staff has been the notion of a key worker. In essence this is a more individualistic approach in which one member of staff gets to know a specific small number of residents well by taking responsibility for assisting in some important areas of everyday life such as helping in bathing, looking after clothes and doing bits of shopping. In the words of an Age Concern guide to setting up and managing a residential home:

Usually a key worker is involved with the new resident from the start. They may visit the resident in their own home and they may help them settle in the residential home. Key workers build up a special relationship with their clients, they know their likes and dislikes, the types of TV and radio programmes they enjoy, when they prefer to get up, how they like their hair done, who their relatives are, and so on. This is likely to add to job satisfaction as well as improving the efficiency and quality of care. (Worsley, 1992, p. 116)

A key worker system has considerable potential not only for making care more personalised but also for facilitating better communication between family caregivers and care staff. Research shows that something that really matters to family caregivers is that care staff acknowledge that they have an insight into the care needs of a resident and are a source of expertise which can contribute to individual care (Duncan and Morgan, 1994). Family caregivers in the current study were asked whether they ever talked to any members of staff about the cared-for person and whether they were aware of any key workers. The amount of interaction reported presents an interesting contrast with hospital-based studies. An evaluation of a hospital rota bed respite care scheme for older people reported that, although half the family caregivers involved made regular visits to the hospital, most reported relatively little contact with staff (Nolan and Grant, 1992). Virtually all the caregivers in the current study, however, reported regularly talking to members of staff about their relative. The matron or manager was a person frequently mentioned. Speaking to staff was very important to most of the family caregivers interviewed. On days when they did not visit, some caregivers made a point of telephoning to ask about the cared-for person.

Key workers were more likely to feature when the cared-for person was in a residential home rather than a nursing home. The notion of key workers is less likely in nursing home settings. Spouses were more likely than daughters or sons to report that the cared-for person did not have a key worker. This is a reflection of greater likelihood of placements being in a nursing home when a spouse has been the main caregiver. It is an interesting reflection on the difficulty of setting up an effective key worker for the system that, although daughters and sons were more likely than spouses to report the existence of a key worker, most had not actually met the care assistant concerned. Many care homes are staffed by part-time workers which makes it particularly difficult for key workers and relatives to meet. There can be no doubt that those family caregivers in contact with a key worker really appreciated having a designated person who took a personal interest in, and had special knowledge of, the cared-for person.

Many of the spouses visiting their partners were themselves old and frail. They were often still deeply upset by a partner's admission to a care home. From their own accounts it was clear that they often turned to care staff for support:

> *There is one nurse that I chat to. She's one of his special nurses. It helps a little, but nobody else can get inside your skin and feel exactly the same as you. But she's interested enough. She lets me talk and that's often enough.* (Wife)

> *They're all very friendly and the manageress always talks to me. If I want to discuss anything about the wife I've only got to ask a nurse and they again said to me, 'If you feel depressed at home give us a ring and come down here and talk to us'.* (Husband)

In conclusion

The family caregivers in the study remained in contact with the cared-for person in the care home. Spouses remained in particularly close contact, half of them visiting five or more times a week. It was not always possible to have any privacy when meeting the cared-for person in the care home. Not surprisingly a lack of privacy caused some caregivers deep distress. Few caregivers regularly shared a meal with the cared-for person in the care home. Being invited to share a meal in the care home was usually a special event such as the day of the cared-for person's admission or Christmas. Approximately one in three daughters or sons reported that their relationship with a parent had improved following the admission to care. In contrast, none of the spouses reported an improved relationship; they themselves tended to feel guilty and the husband or wife now resident often expressed resentment.

The predominant roles for family caregivers are checking up on the quality of care, companionship and handling finances. Very few had any involvement in assisting the cared-for person in practical ways such as shopping or with personal care. Spouses were more likely than daughters or sons to want to continue to help in practical ways but were often discouraged by care staff. Family caregivers were very keen on speaking to care assistants or the manager about the cared-for person when visiting. In some of the residential care homes, the cared-for person was described as having a key worker. Few caregivers, however, reported having met the key worker concerned.

6 Caregivers' views on paying for care

Introduction

One key objective of the research was to explore family caregivers' views on how the costs of care should be met. Family caregivers had direct personal experience of the current system of meeting continuing care costs. Many had had some involvement with community support services while the cared-for person lived at home. All of them had direct experience of paying for long-term care in independent sector homes following the cared-for person's admission, but individuals had different perceptions of this system. This was partly because local differences do exist both between different areas and different local authority employees in how the current system is interpreted (see Chapter 4). Also wide media coverage of some key issues at the time of the fieldwork for the study added to some caregivers' understanding but it also added to the misunderstandings and fears of others.

This chapter begins by looking at caregivers' views on where the financial responsibility for meeting different types of care costs should lie. As using assets and income to pay care costs affects future inheritances, the next section discusses caregivers' views on rights to inheritance in a modern society. The final section describes some of the strategies caregivers reported adopting to avoid the state claiming savings or income to meet long-term care costs.

Views on financial responsibility

Respondents were asked their views on where they thought financial responsibility should lie for meeting the costs of different levels of care. The five levels discussed were:

* minimal support, e.g. two hours' cleaning or housework support per week

- a high level of support, e.g. extensive day and night support

- care in a residential home

- care in a nursing home

- care in an NHS hospital.

Assisted by a showcard specifying potential sources of meeting care costs, i.e. the state, the individual concerned, a spouse or a daughter or son, respondents were asked their reasons for the choices made. Generally caregivers' perceptions of the right balance of responsibility between an individual and the state in paying for care were influenced by the amount of support actually needed.

Minimal support
As far as minimal care, such as two hours' home help, was concerned, family caregivers' views fell into two broad categories. The first was that such support should be totally free regardless of an individual's income or assets and the state should meet the whole cost. Caregivers who were daughters or sons were far more likely to take this view than spouse caregivers. This may have been because spouses were more likely to have been paying directly for services before the cared-for person's admission to a care home. By personally paying they had come to accept such charges as the norm. Most offspring, of course, had not personally had to meet service charges. Those wanting the state to take responsibility argued that older people needed somebody else to do cleaning or shopping only if they themselves were incapacitated by illness. Such costs should, therefore, be borne by the NHS and should be free.

Well basically yes, because they're ill, they are ill, these old dears, and they're not capable of looking after themselves. So it should be free, when you think of it like that. If they weren't ill, they'd be looking after themselves. So they are ill. (Daughter)

Respondents taking this view frequently referred to the dedicated part of the National Insurance contribution:

Because if you've contributed all your life you're entitled at the end of your life to get some pay-back. I feel that all these people who've paid all their working years should have it paid for by the state. (Wife)

I think the local authority should pay because I feel that it is part of the health care that we've paid for with our contributions to the national health, while we worked. (Husband)

The second broad category of response was that most people were capable of paying for a minimal amount of support, such as two hours' home help, without resorting to a local authority or the NHS to meet the costs. A state role should only be residual meeting costs purely for the poor:

If people are able to pay for their own care themselves then I think they should. If somebody can't afford to then I think the local authorities or the state should help them have some kind of dignity at the end of their lives. (Daughter)

I think home help and certain facilities should be paid for privately, if affordable. (Son)

A high level of care at home
As far as an extensive package of support at home was concerned, respondents tended to be sceptical about whether a high level of support from a local authority would ever be forthcoming:

Well, you would not get 24-hour care. The best you could do is four times a day by social services or an agency – morning, lunch, tea and getting them to bed at night. I've never heard of 24-hour care. (Husband)

Several respondents, from their experience of trying to cope with the cared-for person's need for support at home, argued that the problem of obtaining extensive care was so great that people would be better off going into a care home. Virtually everybody agreed that an extensive care package, even if it was forthcoming, would be so expensive that individuals would be unlikely to be able to afford it. The view was widely held that costs should be shared between the state and the individual on the basis of a means-test.

Residential or nursing home care

In contrast to the divided views on responsibility for meeting the costs of a low level of care in the community, family caregivers in the sample, with very few exceptions, took the view that the state should take prime responsibility for meeting residential or nursing home care costs. Other studies and reports indicate that this is a widely held public attitude (Diba, 1996; Joseph Rowntree Foundation, 1996). But, as the House of Commons Health Committee report on long-term care provision and funding commented, despite so many members of society genuinely feeling that the state had reneged on an implicit undertaking to provide long-term care 'it has nevertheless been the case throughout the history of the welfare state that the state has means-tested those people requiring residential social care' (House of Commons Health Committee, 1995/96b, par. 76). Most respondents were critical of means-testing for residential or nursing home care, arguing that both they and the individuals concerned had paid tax and insurance stamps for many years on the assumption that any costs of long-term care would be met in old age.

> *Because you have been paying for it all your life. What are we paying National Health stamps and tax for?* (Wife)

A few caregivers expressed sympathy with the idea that the government was unable to meet the total cost of long-term care:

> *Well, one has to be realistic, and I can't see myself how it is possible for the state to look after everybody that needs the care entirely, because it's a sort of bottomless pit. I mean it's increasingly more difficult to fund, and where is the money coming from?* (Son)

A source of considerable anger was that older people in care homes who had previously lived frugally and saved had to meet care costs from those savings. On the other hand, those who had not saved and had used their money for a good time had their costs met by the state.

Some spouse caregivers expressed resentment at the earlier lack of information about how the costs of long-term care were met. Having to pay towards the costs of care had come as a shock:

Information isn't given; people aren't educated and they come up against it. We never expected this in earlier days, did we? Nobody expected it, this is what's so awful. (Wife)

Care in an NHS hospital
Virtually all caregivers were unanimous that care in NHS hospitals should continue to be free. There was an insistence that a contract existed between the state and the individual because hospital care had been paid for through National Insurance contributions. A typical comment was:

No, I think, if you've paid your stamp every week, it ought to be paid. I paid for a few years. (Husband)

A few respondents, however, conceded that paying hotel costs in a hospital might be acceptable as long as the medical costs remained free.

A daughter's or son's responsibility?
All the caregivers, whether spouses or offspring, were asked whether children should help parents if they became old and frail, and whether any such help should include financial support. Virtually all acknowledged that some responsibility existed; to use Finch's (1995) terminology, there was a vague but definite notion of 'commitments'. In normal circumstances this did not, however, extend to a financial commitment. Many respondents emphasised that children should care about their parents but were doubtful if this should extend to either personally providing actual physical care or to paying for it. Both spouses and adult children tended to argue that there was no filial responsibility to meet care costs of any kind. The greater financial responsibility was seen to lie with the state. The payment of National Insurance contributions was the prime reason given:

I think because Mum worked and paid in all her life: paid her insurances, all her pensions, everything. You know, she's given up all her taxes and everything for all the years she's worked. She's worked very hard. No, I don't feel it should be the responsibility of her children. (Daughter)

That's difficult. I suppose the answer is probably no, the reason being that my generation have always been under the impression that the state looks after you from the cradle to the grave. (Son)

As in Finch and Mason's (1993) study of family obligations, older respondents were less likely than those who were younger to argue that children have a responsibility to care for their parents. Several of the spouses interviewed argued that if anything the obligation was the reverse; parents had a greater obligation to their children than the children had to the parents.

No, I don't think children should be responsible for their parents. I think the parents should be responsible for their children, I really do, because you've had them. But I don't think the children have any choice. (Wife)

Some parents expect their children to look after them and I think it's wrong. I think you are an individual, you bring up your child and you expect them to stand on their own feet – why should you expect them to help keep you in your old age? I really don't think that's fair at all. I think it's all wrong to expect them to contribute. (Wife)

Spouse caregivers were particularly keen to emphasise that their own children's prime responsibility had to be to their own children. Grandparents neither could nor should have priority. Nevertheless in exceptional circumstances the commitment might change. One of the daughters interviewed felt an exceptional obligation towards her mother because of the level of sacrifice which had existed earlier in the relationship:

She looked after me when times were bad. I mean I remember the time, as I told you, she's been divorced 52 years – when I was a baby she divorced her husband. She went out to work in the morning at 5 o'clock and came home at 8 o'clock at night.

Another exceptional circumstance which several respondents thought should change the extent of commitment was if the child concerned was exceptionally wealthy. Lottery winners were considered to have greater responsibility for meeting care costs than those with average incomes.

Views on inheritance

A fundamental expectation in a property-owning democracy like the UK is that children should eventually be able to inherit money and property from their parents. Asserting the right of inheritance has been a significant trigger for major historical political events. A prime example is the barons' revolt against the authority of King John in the thirteenth century fuelled by a demand to be able to leave property to offspring. High on the list of liberties guaranteed in the resulting Magna Carta is the right of inheritance:

> *If any of our earls, barons, or others who hold lands of Us by knight's service shall die, and at the time of his death his heirs shall be of full age and owe a relief, he shall have an inheritance, on payment of ancient relief. If, any such heir shall be underage and a ward, he shall, when he comes of age, have his inheritance without relief or fine.* (Modern translation of Magna Carta: lines 7–9)

In fact, amongst Western democracies, the UK is unusual because people are free to dispose of their property. In many other countries children have a right to a specified portion of their parents' estate (Finch and Wallis, 1993).

Research shows that most inheritances in modern-day Britain pass to close relatives. For example, a random sample of 1,000 wills granted probate in London in 1981 showed that, regardless of estate size, there was a very strong tendency for wealth leavers to keep wealth within the immediate family (Hamnett *et al.*, 1991). A Department of the Environment (DoE) study of house property and inheritance based on the General Household Survey drew the same conclusion (Holmans and Frostega, 1992). Inherited wealth is generally divided between a small number of people. A study of the transfer of property following a death, for example, in the Sheriff's court in Glasgow showed that wealth was divided on average between 2.3 people (Munro, 1988). A high proportion of those who inherit are middle-aged (Munro, 1993) but significant social and economic factors are involved. On the basis of a sample survey of 3,300 respondents, Hamnett (1995b) demonstrated that owner occupiers were six times as likely as council tenants to inherit. The higher the social class, the greater the probability of inheriting housing and the greater the probability of inheriting more than once (Hamnett, 1995b p. 526). Significant geographical factors are also in evidence: people living in the south-east are more likely than those living in the north to inherit (Hamnett, 1995b).

A common assumption in the 1980s was that there would be a significant increase in inherited wealth because of an increase in home ownership and rising house prices. Addressing his first party conference as Prime Minister, John Major famously talked of wealth cascading down through the generations. The evidence is, however, that this has failed to occur. Analysing Inland Revenue statistics Hamnett has demonstrated that the average annual number of estates passing at death to children has not changed in the past 20 years (Hamnett, 1995c). Several factors are implicated. An important one is the increase in housing equity extraction by elderly house owners that in addition to participating in equity release schemes (Mullings and Hamnett, 1992) includes trading down by moving to a cheaper area or house and borrowing on the security of a house without a sale or a move being involved (Holmans, 1991). A further factor is an estimated 30,000 older people selling homes each year to go and live with relatives (Holmans, 1991). Between 32,000 and 40,000 older people each year are further estimated to have to sell their homes to meet the costs of long-term residential or nursing home care (Hamnett, 1995c).

Losing an inheritance

Because a resident's savings are taken into account daughters and sons will forfeit moneys that they might reasonably have expected to inherit when the cared-for person died. Not surprisingly, as most of them administered a parent's moneys, the daughters and sons were only too conscious of the sums involved. Half the daughters and sons in the sample reported that a parent's savings were either currently being used or had already been used down to the statutory limit to pay care home charges. When there had been savings to be used, the mean total used since the parent's admission to a care home was £15,596 and the maximum amount so far used was £44,484. A third of daughters and sons reported that a parent had previously been an owner occupier and in most cases the houses involved had either been sold already or were in the process of being sold.

In the absence of any research directly on affected relatives' perspectives on this phenomenon, family caregivers' views in the present study are particularly interesting. In effect they were contemplating a situation in which their prospects of inheriting from the parent in a care home had either disappeared completely or had been seriously diminished. Their response to a question about whether receiving an inheritance was important to them personally must be interpreted in that light. Approximately half of those who had been disinherited expressed indignation at the current system:

> *Why should I lose my inheritance and other people get away with it? It's wrong, I disagree with the system.* (Son)

The daughters and sons most likely to express indignation were those with children and grandchildren. Those without children were less likely to resent an inheritance being used up in this way:

> *Yes, because I want it to cascade down to my children and grandchildren. I think it's very, very wrong what's happening to me.* (Daughter)

> *Because it would have created wealth for us so that we could then pass it on to our children. We could put it into property.* (Son)

A commonly expressed source of anger was that those people who had not saved got the same quality of care as a parent who had saved and was forced to pay towards care home costs.

Approximately half those who had been disinherited were sanguine about the disappearance of a parent's savings:

*Can I answer that by saying I told my mum, 'If you spend your last
penny on the day you die, good luck to you. We don't want it.'* (Son)

*No, her money is hers. If it's going to make her life more comfortable then
she can have it.* (Daughter)

That such a high proportion of the daughters and sons disinherited did
not appear to be resentful supports Leather and Wheeler's (1988)
argument that attitudes to inheritance are changing because potential
beneficiaries, often in late middle age, are demonstrably able to meet
their own needs.

As far as the spouse caregivers were concerned their ability to leave an
inheritance was under threat because of a partner in a care home. In
addition to the additional costs generated by the admission, several had
seen joint savings diminish because of the local authority's pursuit of a
spouse's liability to maintain (see Chapter 4). An additional inheritance
issue for those who were owner occupiers was what would happen to an
asset such as the house if the spouse living at home died before the
spouse living in long-term care. The replies of spouse caregivers to being
asked how important it was to them personally to be able to leave an
inheritance fell into two broad categories. One was that the person
concerned attached little or no importance to leaving an inheritance:

*No, not at all. My inheritance is what I've given to my children: their
education and their ability to make their own way and make their own
money. If there's anything left over at the end of the day they're quite
entitled to it.* (Husband)

*It's not basically important, but I would rather they had it than the local
authority.* (Wife)

A second was that leaving an inheritance was important but having a
partner in a care home had radically affected the possibility of leaving
one:

*Yes. I think it would be nice to say that you could leave your
grandchildren or whatever something, but it doesn't work out that way*

because you've had to use it all to pay for whatever. I shall come to the time when I shall probably have to pay for home care or whatever, so there's not going to be anything left for the children at all. (Wife)

Evading the system

The right to bequeath an inheritance is an emotive issue. One illustration of the strength of this feeling is the huge upsurge in enquiries to Age Concern England following the production of a briefing paper outlining the advantages and disadvantages of transferring individual assets to intended heirs (House of Commons Health Committee, 1995/96b, par. 298).

All the family caregivers in the sample were asked whether they had ever taken any action to protect an inheritance that they themselves might hope to receive in the future or to ensure that an inheritance might be passed on to their own children. Some respondents had taken action to reduce the impact of the cared-for person's admission to a care home on the inheritance prospects of the next generation. A daughter, for example, having borrowed money from her mother repaid it into an account that was not in her mother's name to avoid the local authority claiming it to meet care costs (see Chapter 4). One of the husbands, when his wife had been admitted to a nursing home, had set about disposing of his property so that if he pre-deceased his wife there would be nothing for her to inherit which could be taken to meet care costs. The matrimonial home had been already made over to one of his daughters and he himself continued to live there as a tenant. Savings had already been put into trust funds for grandchildren. One of the wives whose husband was in a nursing home had taken similar action. She changed her will so that, if she pre-deceased her husband, her half of the house would be inherited by her children. Differences were apparent between caregivers. Most of the spouses seemed to feel powerless to influence their situation. One of the wives commented:

I wouldn't know how to go about it. So you don't do it, and this is something that you don't know about, and by the time you do it's too late. You don't know that these things are going to happen to you, and when they do it's too late, you can't do anything about it.

Many sons and daughters were horrified at a parent's savings diminishing in the care home. It had been brought to their attention in a forcible way that they themselves might one day have to enter residential or nursing home care. Although some felt powerless to challenge the system, most did not. Several had already started to transmit their wealth to their children. One son made sure that his capital remained low enough to avoid inheritance tax:

That involves a mixture of putting things in trust, donating – giving them gifts of money or chattels and planning whereby when the inheritance tax comes there will be the money around to pay for it. I've been very fortunate.

A daughter had invested all her capital in life assurance on the basis that this would ensure that her son would inherit a large sum at his parents' deaths that would not be subject to inheritance tax.

Despite expressing the intention of divesting themselves of savings or income to ensure that these were not forfeit to the state if they themselves had to enter a care home, most offspring had not yet started to do so. On the whole action was being postponed until they reached their sixties or seventies.

We'll make sure the state will keep us. We've been bitten once. It makes you very cynical, very cynical. So if you want your children to actually inherit something, you give it to them – say when we're 60 we'll say, 'Oh here you are – here's a nice nest egg – go and invest it somewhere and we'll have enough money to live on, but you've got your inheritance now'. As long as we live for seven years it's theirs, no questions. We'll give them this house and become tenants. (Daughter)

In conclusion

As far as paying for a minimal amount of support in the community was concerned, family caregivers in the sample were split into two camps. One thought that people should be able to pay a relatively small charge themselves and the other that, as people only needed support because they themselves were ill and infirm, the state had an obligation to provide such support freely. But, when it came to meeting the costs of care in a residential care or nursing home, the views were virtually unanimous. Most respondents thought that such care should be freely available under the NHS. It was considered that those being cared for in care homes had earned free care because of the National Insurance contributions and taxes paid throughout their working lives.

Although spouses, caregivers and daughters and sons considered that children had a moral responsibility to care about their parents, this did not extend to contributing financially to their care costs. An expectation in our type of property-owning society is that children should eventually be able to inherit property and other assets from their parents. Not surprisingly those daughters and sons who had effectively been disinherited by their parents having to pay from savings for their care in a residential or nursing home were often angry. Interestingly, though half of those who had been disinherited were sanguine about the situation, they did not express any resentment. A source of this anger was that their own children were effectively being deprived. Some of the caregivers interviewed had already taken action to prevent themselves being disinherited. Many of the daughters and sons interviewed expressed the intention of taking action in the future to prevent any assets being used if they themselves ever needed to be admitted to a care home.

7 Summary, conclusions and recommendations

Summary

Study aims

The aim of this study was to explore the financial and emotional consequences for family caregivers, spouses and adult children, following the cared-for person's admission to a residential or nursing home. As a small qualitative study it can identify only some of the issues arising from this situation. The sample of 61 family caregivers included 27 spouses (11 husbands and 16 wives) and 34 adult children (24 daughters and ten sons). Selection was through the managers of 35 independent sector nursing and residential care homes. The residents concerned had been admitted since 1 April 1993 when the new system of local authority funding was introduced. All had been assessed as needing care by a local authority.

Background

A key feature of the background to this study is that over half a million older people currently live in long-term institutional care in the UK. The balance of such care has changed radically in recent years. Whereas the majority of older people in this situation used to be looked after in either NHS hospitals or public sector care homes, this is no longer the case. The position is now reversed and, in 1995, 74% of long-term institutional care places were in the independent sector.

In common with other industrialised societies, the UK is experiencing an unprecedented change in its population structure. Increasing numbers of people are now surviving into their eighties and nineties. The social policy significance of these statistics lies in the vulnerability of people of this age. As they are more likely than those who are younger to suffer physical or mental ill-health, the likelihood of an admission to long-term care is greater. Although only 5% of all older people need such care, the proportion rises to approximately one in four of those aged 85 or over.

Bereavement or living alone makes an admission to institutional long-term care more likely but by no means all of those entering care homes are widowed or single. The 1991 Census indicated that just under 50,000 married older men and women were resident in communal establishments in Great Britain. In effect, approximately one in ten people in long-term institutional care are married, usually to a partner living in the community.

The system of paying for long-term care in independent sector care homes is far from straightforward. Since April 1993 local authorities have handled the financial and needs assessments of those wanting state funding. People are entitled to income support at the same level as those remaining in the community and a flat rate residential allowance. Residents have to use their own income and capital to meet fees in addition to the social security benefits to which they may be entitled. In many cases home ownership would be the main source of capital. Capital over £16,000 is regarded as wholly available to meet care costs and between £10,000 and £16,000 is regarded as producing a notional income with contributions being made on a sliding scale. With certain exceptions a property has to be counted as part of a person's capital. If the person living there is a partner, a spouse, a relative over the age of 60 or a relative under the age of 60 who is incapacitated a local authority has to ignore the value of the property.

Spouses are in a different situation from daughters or sons when it comes to financial responsibility. Under Section 42 of the National Assistance Act 1948, a man is liable to maintain his wife and a woman to maintain her husband. This means that when one married partner is admitted to a residential or nursing home a local authority can ask the spouse remaining in the community to contribute towards the costs. Although daughters or sons are not considered liable relatives, they may choose to top up local authority baseline fees if a more expensive care home is preferred.

Choices
Several aspects of choice were discussed with family caregivers including:

- whether there had been adequate support from the statutory services to enable a real choice to be made between the cared-for person remaining at home and entering institutional care

- whether there had been a choice between care homes.

As in other studies there was no doubt that, on the whole, those supported by a spouse tended to be more dependent before admission to a care home than those supported by a son or daughter. Conversely, again as in other studies, when a spouse was the caregiver there was less likely to be support coming into the home from the statutory services. Spouse caregivers were also far more likely to have turned down any support offered. Wives were particularly likely to reject an offer of help with a husband's personal care. On the other hand, a person supported by a spouse was more likely to have day care on at least one day of the week than a person supported by a son or daughter.

An entry to a care home resulted, on the whole, not from a simple progression of increasing dependency but from a major crisis such as an admission to hospital. Two out of three cared-for people entered a care home following a hospital discharge. A family caregiver decision that a care home was appropriate arose from several interrelated factors: a caregiver's own health problems, sleep deprivation, inability to cope with incontinence and inability to cope physically with care tasks. At the point of the interviews, few caregivers thought that the cared-for person could have remained in the community even if there had been more support from the statutory services.

Many family caregivers had felt under pressure to choose a care home swiftly. Half the family caregivers of people discharged from hospital felt they had been put under pressure to find a care home place. The main source of this pressure was hospital staff.

A central theme in good practice guidance is that the older people concerned should be directly involved in the decision to enter care and in a choice between different care homes. Very few of the cared-for people in the present study were reported to have visited the care home before the actual placement. Most family caregivers themselves took responsibility for choosing an appropriate care home and for making choices between individual homes. It was difficult for them to exercise choice about an appropriate care home because of a lack of any relevant previous experience. Most respondents recalled that when setting out to find a suitable care home they had little idea what to expect. When views were held these were largely negative. As few caregivers reported previously discussing the possibility of a care home with the cared-for person before the crisis, there appeared to have been little opportunity to discuss possible preferences.

In a few instances, when a spouse caregiver was particularly frail, a social worker had chosen a care home and made the placement without direct involvement of the caregiver. Some caregivers had firm ideas about an appropriate care home and found somewhere independently without any assistance from a social services department. Although a few caregivers were told to make their selection from a small restricted list of homes, the majority reported being given a complete list of all care homes in the area and being told to set about finding somewhere suitable. The social workers involved usually insisted that they were not allowed to give any advice.

Despite some caregivers managing to visit a large number of care homes, the majority failed to exercise choice in this way and were intimidated by the whole process. A high proportion, half the spouses and one in three offspring, had managed to visit only one care home which was the one in which a placement was subsequently made. Although care home managers are required to produce a brochure or written information under the 1984 Registered Homes Act, only half the family caregivers reported ever obtaining this sort of information.

Two important factors reported as influencing caregivers' choice were location and atmosphere. The proximity to a caregiver's own home was crucial. As far as sons and daughters were concerned a care home had to be within a reasonable car journey time. Wife caregivers needed care homes even closer. Not only did they visit frequently, none of them drove a car and they generally had to pay taxi fares. A good atmosphere was more difficult to define and inevitably meant different things to different people. Many respondents felt there had been little choice

between care homes because placements had to be made fast and
vacancies were few and far between.

Financial consequences for family caregivers
When an older person is admitted to a care home there are likely to be
financial consequences for family caregivers as well as the individual
concerned.

Savings on the cost of care in the community
On the one hand there are likely to be some savings on the costs of
providing care at home. Approximately half of those now in a care home
were reported to have had some support from the statutory services
while living in the community. The charges reported were relatively
modest, a mean of £14.11 per week. Most of the people being cared for
met the charges themselves. A few people had used private services and
the mean charge for support from this source was reported to be £97.14
per week. Only a few daughters and sons living in a different household
from a parent reported personally contributing financially to these costs.

Other costs apart from service charges could be involved. Co-residence
generally seemed to result in a higher expenditure to a family caregiver
than if the cared-for person lived in a separate household. High heating
bills were mentioned by several spouses. Telephone bills could be
another source of high expenditure. A significant indirect cost to several
daughters was giving up paid employment because of a parent's need
for care. All managed to find paid jobs of some kind when the parent
had entered a care home.

*Previous knowledge of the means-tested system of paying long-term
care costs*
Respondents were asked what they had known about paying for care in
a residential or nursing home before the cared-for person's admission.
Although some caregivers said they had always understood that there
would be means-testing, many spouses and offspring reported that they
had assumed that a care home place would be free and paid for by the
NHS. A surprising number of respondents maintained that they had
only really understood the current system of means-testing after the
cared-for person's admission to care. Several wives overwhelmed by

events had given up trying to understand their financial situation, handing pension books, bank accounts and bills over to a son or daughter's management.

Family caregivers do not, in reality, experience an equitable system with national rules and policies. Spouse liability in particular is interpreted in different ways both by individual local authorities and by individual social workers within one authority. Although there is a statutory liability, a spouse's declaration of income is voluntary. Several spouses reported being actively discouraged from declaring savings by a social worker carrying out a local authority assessment. Other spouses, both living in different local authorities and living in the same local authority but with a different social worker, had been encouraged to make a full declaration of income and savings without being made aware that such a declaration was voluntary and, in fact, not in their best interests.

Another complexity frequently misunderstood in the current system is the right to an attendance, or disability living, allowance in a care home if paying privately. A resident is no longer eligible for such an allowance if a local authority accepts financial responsibility but if a resident is self-funding (whether or not there has been a local authority assessment of a need for care) an attendance allowance may be paid. Several daughters and sons reported a parent assessed as needing care by a local authority but being told that savings were currently too high for public funding. No advice was reported in the course of the assessment, however, about the parent's eligibility for an attendance allowance as a self-funder. In effect this meant that capital was run down faster than necessary to meet care costs.

Although the sheer complexity of the system is a barrier to understanding, it is far from being the only one. After years of caregiving, respondents could be too stressed to comprehend what was actually being explained either about care homes or about payment.

The treatment of a married resident's house and savings
Although the value of a house must be taken into account if a resident previously lived alone, a local authority must ignore its value if a spouse is living there. The situation is less straightforward if the spouse

remaining in the community decides to sell the matrimonial home and buy a smaller property. Although Department of Social Security guidance appears to make it clear that a resident's share in the matrimonial home should be ignored in these circumstances, this is not necessarily an interpretation shared by local authorities. One wife who had moved from the matrimonial home to a small flat had been forced to hand half the capital difference to the local authority. Other spouse caregivers interviewed felt unable to move to smaller properties believing that a local authority had placed a charge against the matrimonial home. They had the impression that, regardless of which married partner died first, the property would eventually be forfeit to the local authority.

Misunderstanding capital limits
Two aspects of limits to capital appeared to be misunderstood both by caregivers and by local authority employees. One was the actual level of the capital limits. Several respondents handling the cared-for person's finances had continued to pay towards care costs even though savings were well below the specified limits. Because local authority employees had initially recorded all the financial details and had stated how much had to be paid each week, family caregivers wrongly assumed that they would be notified when the savings had been reduced to the specified limits. The second misunderstanding was the rules in respect of a couple's savings. Income support rules when a couple both live in the community are that the savings limit is the same as for a single person. But if one spouse permanently enters a care home, the couple are treated as two separate single people. Some spouses reported being told by local authority employees that they had to pay from joint savings until these were reduced to the limit specified for a single person.

The cost to spouses
More than one in three of the spouses in the sample were either currently paying care costs from savings or had done so in the past. The sums involved were often large. Taking into account only current payments, the mean amount for those actually contributing was £383 per month with a range from £15 to £1,000.

Topping up local authority payments

Several family caregivers reported that local authority payments were being topped up. The sources for these topping up payments varied. In some instances a charity was topping up but, in others, sons or daughters did so. An agreement to top up the amount a local authority is prepared to pay may cause the relatives concerned great financial hardship if financial circumstances change. The incentive to continue paying a top up is high because a parent will be moved to a care home with a fee at the local authority baseline limit if relatives break their agreement.

Extra costs in the care home

Most family caregivers in the current study handled finances for the cared-for person and were well aware of extra costs. Underwear and night clothes had to be replaced frequently because of the wear and tear entailed in the vigorous care home washing procedures. Although additional costs such as hairdressing were reported in virtually all cases, other costs were idiosyncratic. Incontinence supplies were included in the fees for most people, but several caregivers reported paying extra for them. One wife reported having to pay for her husband's chiropody now that he was in a care home whereas it had been a free service when he lived at home. Just under half the caregivers thought that the personal expenses allowance was adequate for additional expenses. Just over half reported that it was not and they had to meet some of the costs from their own pockets.

Other costs

Two out of three family caregivers reported that the cared-for person moving into a care home had meant extra costs because of the travel involved. Some of the wives reported particularly high costs. They tended to visit frequently but, as none of them was a car driver and care homes were rarely on convenient public transport routes, taxis were often the only means of transport. In these circumstances some of the wives said that the costs were difficult to meet.

Losing an inheritance

Because a resident's savings are taken into account many offspring are effectively disinherited by a parent entering a care home. Not surprisingly as they administered a parent's moneys, most daughters and sons were clear about the sums involved. Over half reported that their parents' savings were either currently being used or had been used in the past to meet care home fees. When a parent had had assets above the specified capital limits, the mean total used since the parent's admission to a care home was £15,596 and the maximum total so far used was £44,484.

A family caregiver's role in the care home
Differences were apparent between spouses and offspring in the frequency of visits to the care home. Most spouses visited five times a week or more frequently and very few visited as little as once a week. Daughters and sons tended to visit less frequently, half visiting weekly and half more frequently. Other differences were evident. Few spouses, for example, had taken their partner out of the care home for an outing since the admission. In contrast most offspring took a parent out at least occasionally for a meal or simply a drive. A key factor was access to a car. None of the wives in the sample drove a car and all relied on public transport or a taxi to visit their husbands in a care home. In any case the level of the dependency of many of these spouses was reported to be high with many having advanced dementia.

Most contact between caregiver and cared-for person took place at the care home. In some homes it was not feasible to meet in private because bedrooms were not suitable venues either because of being too small or because of being shared. Communal lounges were the most frequently mentioned venue. Although these offered welcome distractions to some caregivers, particularly if the resident concerned had little to communicate, other caregivers were very distressed at such public meetings.

Meal-times tend to be significant sociable events in normal family life, but do not tend to be a time when family members are encouraged to interact with a resident in an institutional setting. Although most family caregivers had been offered, and had accepted, tea and biscuits during their visits, few reported regularly having a meal at the care home with the cared-for person. Several spouses, but only two daughters reported regularly sharing a meal at least weekly with the cared-for person in the care home. Some family caregivers had been invited to participate in a meal only on a special occasion, such as Christmas or a wedding anniversary. Although some expressed a wish not to eat at the care home, there were others, particularly spouses, who would have welcomed the opportunity.

Relationship between a caregiver and a cared-for person after the admission to a care home
Differences were apparent between adult children and spouses in respect of reported relationships with the cared-for person after the admission to a care home. Relationships described by daughters and sons generally fell into one of three broad categories:

- a close relationship both before and after admission

- a poor relationship both before and after admission

- an improved relationship following admission.

In contrast none of the spouse caregivers thought there had been any improvement in the relationship with the cared-for person. Although a few thought their relationship had remained good despite a husband or wife's admission, most did not. They described a relationship that had either been, and remained, poor or one that had deteriorated since admission.

A family caregiver's role in the care home
Good practice guidance has relatively little advice to staff on how they should behave towards relatives or on what an appropriate role for those relatives in a care home might be. Few respondents reported continuing to help the cared-for person with personal care. Several spouses reported wanting to continue assisting the cared-for person in a practical way but had been discouraged by staff from doing so at an early stage. Daughters and sons were more likely to make it clear that they were relieved that their involvement in personal care had come to an end.

A prime concern for family caregivers was to ensure that the cared-for person's needs were being met and they monitored the quality of care. Although most caregivers expressed satisfaction with the care home as a whole, no less than half of them found fault with some aspect of care. Shortage of staff was felt to be responsible for many shortcomings such as inadequate stimulation and poor standards of cleanliness. Most caregivers had a role in handling the cared-for person's finances. Few were regularly involved in other practical support such as shopping or doing laundry.

Caregivers' views on paying for care
Caregivers were asked their views on where financial responsibility should lie for meeting different levels of support. These levels of support included two hours' home care per week, an intensive package of care at home, care in a residential or nursing home setting and care in an NHS hospital. As far as paying for a minimal amount of support in the community was concerned, two distinct views were expressed. One was that people should be able to pay a relatively small charge themselves and the other that, as people needed support only because they themselves were ill and infirm, the state had an obligation to provide such support free of charge. Respondents were sceptical about an extensive package of care to a person living at home. Realising the high costs involved, most people considered that the state should take financial responsibility. But, when it came to meeting the costs of care in a residential care or nursing home, views were virtually unanimous. Most respondents thought that such care should be freely available under the NHS. It was considered that those being cared for in residential or nursing homes had earned free care because of National Insurance contributions and taxes paid throughout their working lives.

Although spouse and adult child caregivers considered that children had a moral responsibility to care about their parents, this did not extend to contributing financially to their care costs. If anything spouse caregivers were even more emphatic than offspring. An expectation in our type of property-owning democracy is that children should eventually be able to inherit property and other assets from their parents. Because care costs were met from parental savings a high proportion of the offspring, 50%, had either effectively been disinherited already or were in the process of an inheritance disappearing. Interestingly about half of those who had seen inheritances disappear were phlegmatic about the situation. Half in this situation, on the other hand, were angry. They tended to be parents and grandparents who wanted to pass on an inheritance to the next generation.

A few son and daughter caregivers had taken practical action to prevent themselves being disinherited. An example was a parent's savings being hidden in a child's bank account. Many daughters and sons interviewed expressed the intention of taking action in the future to prevent any assets being used if they themselves ever needed to be admitted to a care home.

Conclusions and recommendations

Did the cared-for person have to move into a care home?
Inevitably given the high cost of a care home place an important question is whether it would have been possible for the cared-for person to have remained at home if there had been additional, or different types of, support available. Some caregivers thought that, with more extensive support from the local authority, this would have been possible. Most family caregivers, however, considered that looking after the cared-for person at home would not have been possible any longer. A retrospective view obviously has all the benefit of hindsight and people are unlikely to conclude that a move into a care home was not the right decision. Nevertheless local authority policies do need careful scrutiny. Because of a perverse financial incentive it appears to be a common practice for local authorities to limit a package of support in the community. In evidence to the House of Commons Health Committee on funding long-term care, the Association of County Councils reported a view that residential or nursing home accommodation was a more economic way of delivering long-term care to people at risk because of economies of scale, mandatory charging and financial assessment rules (House of Commons Health Committee, 1995/96a, par. 40). Assets such as a house could be taken into account by a local authority if a person were admitted to a care home but not if the person received support services at home. In any case the Association stated that it is now a widespread practice for local authorities to limit the cost of a domiciliary care package to the cost of a place in a residential home. In addition it

seems that many local authority social workers are doing a benefits check at the time of means-testing for the care charges with the result that attendance allowance take-up is increasing.

The issues are, of course, wider than cost. A significant research finding was that spouse caregivers were more likely than non-resident daughters and sons to be looking after people with high dependency but conversely were less likely to have support services coming into the home. Logistical and practical problems exist in providing the type and level of support needed, particularly if the cared-for person is co-resident with the family caregiver. When a person needs extensive and frequent personal care throughout the day it is difficult for a home care service to match that need. A major problem for people whether living alone or co-resident with a caregiver was the inappropriate timing of so much home care. Frequent caregiver complaints were that home care staff often came far too early in the evening to assist the cared-for person to go to bed. This destroyed the opportunity to do other things in the evening. Conversely there were complaints that staff arrived very late in the morning so that the cared-for person remained bored in bed for long periods. When so many complaints of this nature emerge, questions are raised about how a service is organised. Obviously it is difficult to employ sufficient staff to allow service users to have support at the time wanted. Nevertheless a larger workforce of part-time staff first thing in the morning and last thing at night may prove far more satisfactory to service users than a small number of full-time staff who work longer hours. If a service results in a person having to remain in bed for inordinate lengths of time, it may be so demoralising that entry to a care home may seem preferable. The development of a service providing people with support at times when they need it remains an important service delivery goal.

Could a rehabilitation scheme have enabled people discharged from hospital to return to their own homes?
A high proportion of those being cared for had entered care following a discharge from hospital. Many of the caregivers involved felt under pressure to arrange an admission to a care home place as soon as possible. If rehabilitation had been available, either in a hospital setting

or in a scheme that was halfway between institutional care and care at home, it is possible that some of those being cared for could have returned home.

Family caregivers need more support and information when choosing a care home
As we have seen, despite several years' involvement in supporting a dependent person in the community, most family caregivers appeared to have given little prior consideration to exploring any long-term care options. Many started their search with a negative image of a care home. Uncertain about what different types of care homes existed they were issued with a basic list of names, addresses and telephone numbers by social workers who insisted they had no role in giving advice. A conclusion drawn from an SSI study of hospital discharge that in some instances the needs of carers and users may be better protected by a more active social service department involvement seems to under-rate the difficulties of many family caregivers in this situation (Department of Health\SSI, 1995, p. 29).

Few members of the public know much about care homes and family caregivers are no exception. An understanding of the fundamental aspects of long-term care is a prerequisite to exercising meaningful choice. Key aspects of the system which need to be understood are:

- the difference between a residential and a nursing home

- the relationship between a local authority and the independent sector

- the different broad types of care homes, e.g. care homes with large communal facilities and one lounge and dining room common to all residents are different from other homes with small group living units which have separate kitchens and dining rooms for small groups of residents

- a key worker system exists in some care homes and individual members of staff take responsibility for getting to know individual residents and assisting them with specific activities.

A National Consumer Council (1995) study of local authority policies and practice in charging consumers for services pointed out that many local authorities assume that the attendance allowance and the disability living allowance are available to pay for the services arranged. The net effect in those authorities is that encouraging benefit take-up increases the amount recouped from the consumers.

If the cared-for person suffers from dementia there are choices to be made between different types of care homes:

- a care home may be for dementia sufferers only

- a special unit for dementia sufferers may exist within a general care home

- a care home may have a locked front door to restrict dementia sufferers who wander but it may not

- a care home may have certain design features specifically to help dementia sufferers to find their way around.

If social workers find it difficult or inappropriate to explain the complexities of the care home system, other ways of conveying basic information need to be found. These might include written information in the form of a booklet, a video which would have the advantage of showing the interiors of different care homes or a local discussion group for caregivers currently examining the local options.

In addition to good background information, family caregivers needed specific up-to-date information about current vacancies when trying to find a suitable care home. A conclusion in the Department of Health/SSI (1995) study of hospital discharge that there was a dearth of information about provision in the independent and public sectors and an absence of up-to-date information on availability can only be echoed in the current study. Many family caregivers had only ever visited one care home and accepted the first vacancy because it was difficult to get a complete picture of local vacancies.

Caregivers feel satisfied with care in the homes as a whole
Much research on care homes emphasises negative aspects of the care as
the titles demonstrate, e.g. *The Last Refuge* (Townsend, 1962), *Taken for a
Ride* (Meacher, 1972), *Private Lives in Public Places* (Willcocks *et al.*, 1987).
A main conclusion from the current research is that, although concern
was often expressed about certain aspects of the care, most family
caregivers expressed high levels of satisfaction with the quality of the
care home. Spouses were particularly likely to express satisfaction.

Supporting the relationship between a family caregiver and a resident
Staff in a residential or nursing care home have a responsibility towards
a family caregiver as well as the person who has become resident. Many
spouse caregivers interviewed were obviously deeply distressed at a
partner's admission to a care home and needed support themselves to
cope with a sense of guilt and failure because they had been unable to
continue coping at home. Although most offspring made it clear that
they were relieved to have no further involvement in practical care, this
was far from the case with a number of the spouses. They had, after all,
usually clocked up years of experience in helping partners with all sorts
of personal care. As we have seen, care staff could be very discouraging
to family caregivers who wanted to assist in practical ways. Conversely,
of course, the main complaint that caregivers had about the care homes
was that they were often short staffed. It is important to the wellbeing of
family caregivers, those who are being cared for and care staff, who are
often under a lot of work pressure, to review the ways in which family
caregivers might continue to be involved in some aspects of care.
Negotiating a written contract between care staff and a family caregiver
may assist in establishing clarity about responsibilities for assisting in
certain areas of life.

A need for privacy
As we have seen, many family caregivers lack an opportunity to meet
the cared-for person in private. Although some of those being cared for
are taken out by relatives, this is not always possible, particularly if the
family caregiver lacks a car or the cared-for person is too disabled
physically or is too confused to leave the care home. It is important to
develop facilities which enable family meetings to be private. If
bedrooms are too small or inappropriate, a separate sitting room from

the communal lounge for the use of a resident and visitors needs to be set up.

Meal-times are generally socially important to family members. It should be possible for a care home to cater for a family caregiver with advance notice and payment for the meal. Some family members will never want to do this. They may only be able to visit at times other than meal-times or they may find it difficult to enjoy a meal if the cared-for person or other residents have developed unacceptable table manners. If the cared-for person generally needs staff attention to eat a meal, a relative could provide assistance and release staff time. Being encouraged to take occasional meals in the care home would be particularly significant for some of the spouse caregivers.

Lack of equitable treatment in paying towards residential and nursing home costs

The current government is committed to review the current system of paying for long-term care and a Royal Commission is reviewing future options. The current system has many anomalies, and lack of equity in the current arrangements at all levels has led to many people in our society having a strong sense of injustice. Some people needing long-term care receive it virtually free in NHS hospitals or in nursing homes paid for by health authorities. Although pensions and social security benefits are affected after a time, the person involved does not have to utilise assets. Most people needing long-term care enter independent sector nursing homes or independent or public sector residential homes. People who have savings and who have higher income receive the same care but have to pay for it. If Age Concern England's volume of enquiries about disposal of assets is a valid indicator, many older people are now investigating how to dispose of their assets so that their children rather than the state will benefit (Joseph Rowntree Foundation, 1996, p. 23). Although only a small number of family caregivers interviewed for the present study were prepared to admit they had taken direct action to prevent the cared-for person's assets being used, many of those with children said they had every intention of passing on assets before they reached the age when long-term care might be needed. It is not surprising in a property-owning democracy that people think it is very important to pass on an inheritance to their children. Family caregivers in the study who were angry at the cared-for person's savings being used to meet care costs expressed anger at being deprived of the opportunity to eventually use the assets for the benefit of their own children.

Maladministration
Many family caregivers handling residents' finances are uncertain about the rules concerning capital limits. They assume that the local authority will notify them when savings have been reduced to the limit. As the research has shown, this may not happen. Several respondents had continued to pay care costs when savings had gone below the limits. It is very important for local authorities to have an effective system to notify the person handling a resident's finances when savings are getting near the specified limits.

The inequitable treatment of spouses
A spouse's situation under the current system is in urgent need of review and reform. Currently a spouse as a liable relative under the law has a financial obligation to a partner whether that person is in the community or long-term residential or nursing home care. In marked contrast a person who is cohabiting and has not entered a marriage contract has no such obligation. Although there have been significant changes in the treatment of occupational and private pensions, with the spouse in long-term care now able to give half a pension to a spouse remaining in the community, salient financial issues remain. As far as income is concerned, wives remaining in the matrimonial home may experience financial difficulties. A husband is more likely than a wife to have an occupational pension and even if a wife has an occupational pension in her own right it is likely to be less than her husband's. Half a husband's occupational pension being taken to pay for his care does not alter the fact that the wife still has household bills coming in. Although some of these bills may be less because there is now one person in a household, many such as a TV licence, water rates, telephone, and heating and cooking bills are likely to remain the same. As we have seen many spouses visit their partner in a care home very frequently. None of the wives in the study actually drove a car so the costs of visiting the care home could be quite high, particularly if the care home was not on a public transport route and taxis had to be used. As it is usually

important for both the spouse remaining at home and the spouse living in a care home that there should be such frequent visiting, this is an important issue. One way of addressing this issue might be a travel allowance. Another way would be to extend transport schemes staffed by volunteers to spouses in this situation.

As far as assets are concerned, this research indicated that spouses in similar circumstances had quite different experiences. Individual local authorities had their own interpretations and individual social workers working in those organisations also made decisions about whether or not to implement the rules. Consequently some spouses had to pay out large amounts each week from savings towards the cost of a partner's care and other spouses in very similar financial situations paid nothing.

A spouse's right to property is also being subject to widely different interpretations. It must be common for a spouse remaining at home in the community to decide to move to a smaller property after a partner has been admitted to a care home. There may be a mix of motives for such a move, including moving from property that serves as a constant reminder of the absent partner. But, as this study has shown, in some areas a local authority will claim half the capital difference when in other areas this would not be the case.

The rights of spouses when they want to move home in this way need urgent review. It is unacceptable that there are such different interpretations of rights in different parts of the country. Many of those older people remaining in the community after a partner has been admitted to a care home are exceptionally vulnerable. They feel guilty because they have been unable to continue caring at home, and they are often themselves very old and may be also physically or mentally frail. For many challenging a bureaucratic decision would not be feasible. It is important to ensure that their rights are respected and that individual local authorities do not pursue policies which are contrary to the intention of central government guidance.

A need for information about the current system of paying for care
Family caregivers and those they are caring for need more information about the system of paying for care. Although some had realised that

means-testing determined whether the costs of care home places had to be met relatively early in the process, for many the knowledge that the NHS would not meet the care costs came as a shock. It may be difficult to take in verbal explanations in the course of the trauma of sorting out an admission to a care home. In any case the system is so complex that the many issues would not be covered in one explanation. It is important that more written information about the system of charging is available at an early stage in the process for family caregivers. As the research showed, mistakes do happen. Residents' savings do go down below the capital limits and caregivers do fail to help the cared-for person claim relevant social security benefits.

In conclusion

Daughters, sons, husbands and wives continue to care a great deal about the wellbeing of a relative who has been admitted to a care home. This study shows that they need far more information and support in choosing an appropriate care home. Most family caregivers had little previous experience of care homes and a positive message of the research is that a high level of satisfaction was generally expressed about the care home. It is important to explore ways in which those family caregivers wanting to continue giving some practical care to a cared-for person can be encouraged to do so. Spouses, in particular, may both want and need to give practical support to a partner. Care staff need to think about encouraging rather than discouraging involvement. The issue of individuals meeting their own care costs remains a fraught one. Although some daughters and sons are phlegmatic about disinheritance, others are angry about the current system and disillusioned about the welfare state. A common threat of people in this situation, to ensure that they themselves will disperse wealth to their own children rather than meet their own costs in a care home, is not one to take lightly. Spouse liability is a controversial concept in need of urgent review. It is surely unacceptable that those who enter a marriage contract are financially penalised while those who cohabit are not. The arbitrary nature of local authority interpretation and implementation of spouse liability makes this an important area to review on a national basis.

References

Age Concern England (1995a) *Briefings: NHS Responsibilities for Continuing Care, Health and Hospital Discharge Arrangements.* London: Age Concern England

Age Concern England (1995b) *Briefings: Information about Transfer of Assets by Older People with Respect to Local Authority Charging Procedures for Residential and Nursing Home Care.* London: Age Concern England

Age Concern England (1996a) *Paying for Residential and Nursing Home Fees from Income Support and Attendance Allowance.* London: Age Concern England

Age Concern England (1996b) *Liable Relatives, Occupational Pensions and Paying for Care in a Residential or Nursing Home.* London: Age Concern England

Age Concern England (1996c) *Briefings: Pensioners' Incomes.* London: Age Concern England

Age Concern England (1996d) *Resident's Money: A Guide to Good Practice in Care Homes.* London: Age Concern England

Allan, G. (1988) 'Kinship, responsibility and care for elderly people', *Ageing and Society*, No. 8, pp. 249–68

Allen, I. and Perkins, E. (1995) 'Discussion', in I. Allen and E. Perkins (eds) *The Future of Family Care for Older People.* London: HMSO

Allen, I., Hogg, D. and Peace, S. (1992) *Elderly People, Choice, Participation and Satisfaction.* London: Policy Studies Institute

Alzheimer's Disease Society (1997) *Relatives' Views of Residential and Nursing Home Care: A Survey.* London: Alzheimer's Disease Society

Arber, S. and Ginn, J. (1991) *Gender and Later Life. A Sociological Analysis of Resources and Constraints*. London: Sage Publications

Askham, J. and Thompson, C. (1990) *Dementia and Home Care*. Age Concern Institute of Gerontology Research Paper No. 4. London: Age Concern England

Askham, J., Hancock, R. and Hills, J. (1995) *Opinions on Pensions. Older People's Attitudes to Incomes, Taxes and Benefits*. London: Age Concern Institute of Gerontology

Askham, J., Barry, C., Grundy, E., Hancock, R. and Tinker, A. (1992) *Life After 60*. London: Age Concern Institute of Gerontology

Association of County Councils (1993) *Commissioning Care: A Survey of Fee Negotiations with Independent Homes for Older People*. London: Association of County Councils Publications

Association of County Councils (1995) *Negotiating Fees*. London: Associations of County Councils Publications

Association of Directors of Social Services Evidence to House of Commons Health Committee (1995/96) *Long-term Care: Future Provision and Funding*. Vol. 11. London: HMSO

Audit Commission (1986) *Making a Reality of Community Care*. London: HMSO

Audit Commission (1992) *Community Care: Managing the Cascade of Change*. London: HMSO

Audit Commission (1996) *Balancing the Care Equation: Progress with Community Care*. London: HMSO

Baldwin, S. (1995) 'Love and money: the financial consequences of caring for an older relative', in I. Allen and E. Perkins (eds) *The Future of Family Care for Older People*. London: HMSO

Baldwin, S. and Lunt, N. (1996) *Charging Ahead: Local Authority Charging Policies for Community Care.* Bristol: Policy Press

Bartlett, H. (1993) *Nursing Homes for Elderly People: Questions of Quality and Policy.* Switzerland: Harwood Academic Publishers

Bartlett, H. and Challis, L. (1985) 'Constraints on care: supplementary benefit, the elderly and the private sector', *Social Services Research*, No. 5, pp. 27–35

Benefits Agency (1996) *A Guide to Income Support.* Leaflet 1520. London: Benefits Agency and Central Office of Information

Bland, R., Bland, R., Cheetham, J., Lapsley, I. and Llewellyn, S. (1992) *Residential Homes for Elderly People. Their Costs and Quality.* London: HMSO

Bone, M., Gregory, J., Gill, B. and Larder, D. (1992) *Retirement and Retirement Plans.* London: HMSO

Bradshaw, J. (1988) 'Financing private care for the elderly', in S. Baldwin, G. Parker and R. Walker (eds) *Social Security and Care.* Avebury: Gower

Brearley, C. P. (1990) *Working in Residential Homes for the Elderly.* London: Routledge

Brody, E., Dempsey, M. and Pruchno, N. P. (1990) 'Mental health of sons and daughters of the institutionalised aged', *The Gerontologist*, Vol. 30, No. 2, pp. 212–19

Bronsbury L. (1995) 'The legal framework', in S. Balloch and G. Robertson (eds) *Charging for Social Care 1995.* London: Local Authority Anti-Poverty Research Unit

Buckwalter, K. and Hall, G. (1987) 'Families of the institutionalized older adult: a neglected resource', in T. Brubacker (ed.) *Aging, Health and Family: Long-Term Care.* Newbury Park: Sage

Central Statistical Office (1995) *Social Trends 25*. London: HMSO

Central Statistical Office (1996) *Social Trends 26*. London: HMSO

Central Statistical Office (1997) *Social Trends 27*. London: HMSO

Centre for Policy on Ageing (1984) *Home Life*. London: CPA

Centre for Policy on Ageing (1996) *A Better Home Life*. London: CPA

Chester, R. and Davies, S. (1996) *Appetite for Life*. London: Counsel and Care

Coleman, P. (1990) 'Adjustment in later life', in J. Bond and P. Coleman (eds) *Ageing in Society: An Introduction to Social Gerontology*. London: Sage Publications

Corden, A. (1992) 'Setting fees in private homes: some reasons why they vary so much', in J. Morton (ed.) *Financing Elderly People in Independent Sector Homes: The Future. Ageing Update Conference Proceedings*. London: Age Concern Institute of Gerontology

Counsel and Care (1991) *Not Such Private Places*. London: Counsel and Care

Department of Health (1994a) *Private Hospitals, Homes and Clinics Registered under Section 23 of the Registered Homes Act 1984*. London: Government Statistical Service

Department of Health (1994b) *Charges for Residential Accommodation*. LAC (94) 1

Department of Health (1994c) *Residential Accommodation for Elderly and for Younger Physically Disabled People – Year Ending 31 March 1993*. London: Government Statistical Service

Department of Health (1996) *Moving into a Care Home, Things You Need To Know*. London: Department of Health

Department of Health\SSI (1989) *Homes are for Living in.* London: HMSO

Department of Health\SSI (1990) *Caring for Quality: Guidance on Standards for Residential Homes for Elderly People.* London: HMSO

Department of Health\SSI (1995a) *Moving On.* London: DoH

Department of Health\SSI (1995b) *Moving On: A Further Year.* London: DoH

Department of Social Security (1994) *Income-related Benefits – Estimates of Take-up in 1993/94.* London: DSS

Department of Social Security (1995a) *The Charges for Residential Accommodation Guidance.* London: DSS

Department of Social Security (1995a) *Income Support Statistics. Residential Care and Nursing Home Report.* London: DSS Analytical Services Division

Department of Social Security (1995b) *The Law Relating to Social Security Supplement No. 37.* London: DSS

Department of Social Security (1996a) *Income Support Statistics: Quarterly Enquiry May 1995.* London: DSS Analytical Services Division

Department of Social Security (1996b) *Social Security Statistics.* London: HMSO

Diba, R. (1996) *Meeting the Costs of Continuing Care: Public Views and Perception.* York: York Publishing Services

Dimond, B. (1997) *Legal Aspects of Care in the Community.* Basingstoke: Macmillan Press

Duncan, M. T. and Morgan, D. L. (1994) 'Sharing the caring: family caregivers. Views of their relationships with nursing home staff', *The Gerontologist*, Vol. 34, No. 2, pp. 234–44

Edwards, P. and Kenny, D. (1995) *A Survey of Fee Negotiations with Independent Homes for Older People*. London: Association of County Councils

Fimister, G. (1995) *Social Security and Community Care in the 1990s*. Sunderland: Business Education Publishers Limited

Finch, J. (1995) 'Responsibilities, obligations and commitments', in I. Allen and E. Perkins (eds) *The Future of Family Care for Older People*. London: HMSO

Finch, J. and Groves, D. (1983) *A Labour of Love: Women, Work and Caring*. London: Routledge and Kegan Paul

Finch, J. and Mason, J. (1993) *Negotiating Family Responsibilities*. London: Routledge

Finch, J. and Wallis, L. (1993) 'Inheritance, care bargains and elderly people's relationship with their children', in D. Challis and B. Davies (eds) *Health and Community Care: UK and International Perspectives*. Aldershot: Gower

Gibbs, I. and Oldman, C. (1993) *Housing Wealth in Later Life a Mixed Blessing*. York: Centre for Housing Policy

Gladstone, J. W. (1995) 'Elderly married persons living in long-term care institutions: a qualitative analysis of feelings', *Ageing and Society*, pp. 493–511

Glendinning, C. (1992) *The Costs of Informal Care*. London: HMSO

Grau, L., Teresi, J., Burton, B. and Chandler, B. (1995) 'Family members' perception of the quality of nursing home care', *International Journal of Geriatric Psychiatry*, Vol. 10, pp. 787–96

Grundy, E. (1995a) *Evidence to House of Commons Health Committee. Long-term Care Funding: Future Provision and Funding*. Vol. 11. London: HMSO

Grundy, E. (1995b) 'Demographic influences on the future of family care', in I. Allen and E. Perkins (eds) *The Future of Family Care for Older People*. London: HMSO

Hall, B. I. (1989) 'The role of adult children in helping chronically ill hospitalised parents', *Canadian Journal on Aging*, Vol. 8, No. 1, pp. 68–78

Hamnett, C. (1995a) *Inheritance in Britain: the Disappearing Billions*. London: PPP Lifetime plc

Hamnett, C. (1995b) 'A nation of inheritors? Housing inheritance wealth and inequality in Britain', *Journal of Social Policy*, Vol. 20, pp. 509–36

Hamnett, C. (1995c) 'Equity release and inheritance', in I. Allen and E. Perkins (eds) *The Future of Family Care for Older People*. London: HMSO

Hamnett, C., Harmer, M. and Williams, P. (1991) *Safe as Houses*. London: Paul Chapman Publishing Ltd

Hancock, R. and Jarvis, C. (1994) *The Long-term Effects of Being a Carer*. London: HMSO

Hancock, R. and Weir, P. (1994) *More Ways than Means. A Guide to Pensioners' Incomes in Great Britain during the 1980s*. London: Age Concern Institute of Gerontology

Henwood, M. and Wistow, G. (1995) *The 'Loophole' Route into Residential Care*. Personal Social Service Research Unit & Nuffield Institute of Health Mixed Economy of Care Bulletin no. 3, pp. 20–2

Holmans, A. (1991) *Estimates of Housing Withdrawal by Owner Occupiers in the UK 1970 to 1990*. Government Economic Service Working Paper, No. 116, November

Holmans, A. and Frostega, M. (1992) *House Property and Inheritance in the UK*. London: HMSO, Department of the Environment

House of Commons (1996) *Hansard* 12 March, Cols 597–600

House of Commons Health Committee (1995/96a) *Third Report Vol. 1 Long-term Care: Future Funding and Provision*. Vol. 133. London: HMSO

House of Commons Health Committee (1995/96b) *Long-term Care: Future Funding and Provision*. Vol. 11. HMSO: London

Howarth, G. (1993) 'Food consumption, social roles and personal identity', in S. Arber and M. Evandrou (eds) *Ageing, Independence and the Life Course*. London: Jessica Kingsley Publications

Howe Report (1992) *The Quality of Care: Report of the Residential Care Inquiry*. London: Local Government Board

Hutton, S. (1996) 'Progress report. Current and future incomes for older people', *Ageing and Society*, Vol. 16, pp. 775–87

Jarvis, C., Hancock, R., Askham, J. and Tinker, A. (1996) *Getting around after 60*. London: HMSO

Joseph Rowntree Foundation Inquiry (1996) *Meeting the Costs of Continuing Care*. York: Joseph Rowntree Foundation

Kahana, E., Kahan, B. and Young, R. (1985) 'Social factors in institutional living', in W. Peterson and J. Quadango (eds) *Social Bonds in Later Life: Aging and Independence*. Beverley Hills, CA: Sage

Kane, R. A. and Kane, R.L. (1987) *Long-term Care: Principles, Programmes and Policies*. New York: Springer

Kenny, D. (1997) *Influencing the Market: Negotiating Fees with Independent Homes*. London: Local Government Association

Kenny, D. and Edwards, P. (1995) *From Social Security to Community Care: the Impact of the Transfer of Funding on Local Authorities*. London: London Research Centre

Kitwood, T., Buckland, S. and Petre, T. (1995) *Brighter Futures*. Oxford: Anchor Publications

Laing and Buisson (1995) *Care of Elderly People – Market Survey*. London: Laing & Buisson Publications

Laing, W. (1993) *Financing Long-term Care: the Crucial Debate*. London: Age Concern England

Laing, W. (1998) *A Fair Price for Care? Disparities between Market Rates and State Funding of Residential Care*. York: JRF

Leather, P. and Wheeler, R. (1988) *Making use of Home Equity in Old Age*. London: Building Societies Association

Levin, E., Sinclair, I. and Gorbach, P. (1989) *Families, Services and Confusion in Old Age*. Avebury: Gower

Levin, E., Moriarty, J. and Gorbach, P. (1994) *Better for the Break*. London: HMSO

Lewis, J. and Meredith, B. (1988) *Daughters Who Care*. London: Routledge and Kegan Paul

Martin, J., White, A. and Meltzer, H. (1989) *Disabled Adults: Services, Transport and Employment*. OPCS Survey of Disability, Report 4. London: HMSO

Meacher, M. (1972) *Taken for a Ride*. London: Longman

Medical Research Council (1994) *The Health of the UK's Elderly People*. London: MRC

Meredith, B. (1995a) 'The ways and means of charging', in S. Balloch and G. Robertson (eds) *Charging for Social Care 1995*. London: Local Authority Anti-Poverty Research Unit

Meredith, B. (1995b) *The Community Care Handbook: the Reformed System Explained*. London: Age Concern England

Montgomery, R., Stull, D. and Borgata, E. (1985) 'Measurement and analysis of burden', *Research on Aging*, Vol. 7, pp. 137–52

Mullings, B. and Hamnett, C. (1992) 'Equity release schemes and equity extraction by elderly households in Britain', *Ageing and Society*, Vol. 12, pp. 413–41

Munro, M. (1988) 'Housing wealth and inheritance', *Journal of Social Policy*, Vol. 17, pp. 417–36

Munro, M. (1993) 'Housing costs and assets', in T. Warnes (ed.) *Homes and Travel: Local Life in the Third Age*. Carnegie Enquiry into the Third Age

Murphy, E. (1986) *Dementia and Mental Illness in the Old*. London: Papermac

National Consumer Council (1995) *Charging Consumers for Social Services: Local Authority Policy and Practice*. London: National Consumer Council

National Institute for Social Work (1988) *Residential Care for Elderly People*. London: NISW

Neill, J., Sinclair, I., Gorbach, P. and Williams, J. (1988) *A Need for Care? Elderly Applicants for Local Authority Homes*. Avebury: Gower

Netten, A. (1993) *A Positive Environment?* Ashgate: PSSRU University of Kent

Nolan, M. and Grant, G. (1992) *Regular Respite: an Evaluation of a Hospital Rota Bed Scheme for Elderly People*. ACIOG research paper No. 6. London: Age Concern Institute of Gerontology

Nolan, M., Grant, G. and Keady, J. (1996) *Understanding Family Care*. Buckingham: Open University Press

Norman, A. (1984) *Bricks and Mortals: Design and Lifestyles in Old People's Homes*. London: CPA

OECD (1996) *Caring for Frail Elderly People*. Policies in Evolution, Social Policy Studies, No. 17. Paris: OECD

Office of National Statistics (1997) *Social Trends 1997*. London: The Stationery Office

Office of Population, Census and Surveys (1993) *1991 Census: Communal Establishments*. London: HMSO

Oldman, C. (1991) *Paying for Care: Personal Sources of Funding for Care*. York: Joseph Rowntree Foundation

Oldman, C., Quilgars, D. and Carlisle, J. (1998) *Living in a Home*. Oxford: Anchor Research

Opit, L. and Pahl, J. (1993) 'Institutional care for elderly people: can we predict admissions?', *Research, Policy and Planning*, pp. 10–15

Parker, G. (1993) *With this Body: Caring and Disability in Marriage*. Buckingham: Open University Press

Parker, H. (1997) *Money to Spend as They Wish: The Personal Expenses Allowance in Care Homes*. London: Age Concern England

Parker, R. (1990) 'Care and the private sector', in I. Sinclair, R. Parker, D. Leat and J. Williams (eds) *The Kaleidoscope of Care*. London: HMSO

Parris Stephens, M., Crowther, J., Hobfoll, S. and Tennenbaum, D. (1990) *Stress and Coping in Later-life Families*. London: Hemisphere Publishing Corporation

Peace, S., Kellaher, L. and Willcocks, D. (1997) *Re-evaluating Residential Care*. Buckingham: Open University Press

Phillips, J. (1992) *The Admission Process into Private Residential Care Homes*. Avebury: Gower

Pratt, C., Schmall, V. and Wright, S. (1987) 'Ethical concerns of family caregiving to dementing patients', *The Gerontologist*, Vol. 25, No. 5, pp. 632–8

Qureshi, H. and Simons, K. (1987) 'Resources within families caring for elderly people', in J. Brannen and G. Wilson (eds) *Give and Take in Families*. London: Allen and Unwin

Qureshi, H. and Walker, A. (1989) *The Caring Relationship: Elderly People and their Families*. Basingstoke: Macmillan Education Ltd

Relatives Association (1993) *Relatives' Views*. London: Relatives Association

Ritchie, K. and Ledesert, B. (1992) 'The families of the institutionalised dementing elderly: a preliminary study of stress in a French care-giver population', *International Journal of Geriatric Psychiatry*, Vol. 7, pp. 5–14

Roberts, S., Steele, J. and Moore, N. (1991) *Finding out about Residential Care: Result of a Survey of Users*. London: Policy Studies Institute

Rosenthal, C. J. and Dawson, P. (1991) 'Wives of institutionalised elderly men. The first stage of transition to quasi widowhood', *Journal of Ageing and Health*, Vol. 3, No. 3, pp. 315–34

Rosenthal, C., Sulman, J. and Marshall, V. (1993) 'Depressive symptoms in family caregivers', *The Gerontologist*, Vol. 33, No. 2, pp. 249–57

Rubin, A. and Shuttlesworth, G. (1983) 'Engaging families as support resources in nursing home care: ambiguity in the subdivision of tasks', *The Gerontologist*, Vol. 23, No. 6, pp. 632–6

Schwartz, A. and Vogel, M. (1990) 'Nursing home staff and residents' families role expectations', *The Gerontologist*, Vol. 30, No. 1, pp. 49–53

Secretaries of State for Health, Social Security, Wales and Scotland (1989) *Caring for People: Community Care in the Next Decade and Beyond*. Cmnd 849. London: HMSO

Secretary of State for Health (1996) *A New Partnership for Care in Old Age*. Cmnd 3242. London: HMSO

Shuttlesworth, G., Rubin, A. and Duffy, M. (1982) 'Families versus institutions: incongruent role expectations in the nursing home', *The Gerontologist*, Vol. 22, No. 2, pp. 200–8

Sinclair, I. (1988) 'Residential care', in I. Sinclair, R. Parker, D. Leat and J. Williams (eds) *The Kaleidoscope of Care*. London: HMSO

Skaff, M. and Pearlin (1992) 'Caregiving: role engulfment and loss of self', *The Gerontologist*, Vol. 32, No. 5, pp. 656–64

Smith, K. and Bengston, V. (1979) 'Positive consequences of institutionalisation: solidarity between elderly parents and their middle-aged children', *The Gerontologist*, Vol. 19, pp. 438–47

Smith, G. and Cantley, C. (1985) *Assessing Health Care: A Study in Organisational Evaluation*. Buckinghamshire: Open University Press

SSI/ DH/ National Health Executive (1994) *The F Factor*. London: Department of Health

Tinker, A., McCreadie, C., Wright, F. and Salvage, A. (1994) *The Care of Frail Elderly People in the United Kingdom*. London: HMSO

Townsend, A. (1990) 'Nursing home care and family caregivers' stress', in M. Stephens, J. Crowther, S. Hobfoll and D. Tennenbaum (eds) *Stress and Coping in Later-life Families*. London: Hemisphere Publishing Corporation

Townsend, P. (1962) *The Last Refuge*. London: Routledge and Kegan Paul

Twigg, J. (1992) *Carers Research and Practice*. London: HMSO

Twigg, J. and Atkin, K. (1994) *Carers Perceived: Policy and Practice in Informal Care*. Buckingham: Open University Press

Twigg, J., Atkin, K. and Perring, C. (1990) *Carers and Services: A Review of Research.* London: HMSO

Wagner, G. (1988) *A Positive Choice.* London: HMSO

Weaver, T., Willcocks, D. and Kellaher, L. (1985) *The Business of Care: A Study of Private Residential Homes for Elderly People.* Research Report No. 1. London: Centre for Environmental and Social Studies in Ageing, Polytechnic of North London

Wenger, C. (1984) *The Supportive Network: Coping with Old Age.* London: Allen and Unwin

Wenger, C. (1990) 'Elderly carers – the need for appropriate intervention', *Ageing and Society*, Vol. 10, No. 2, pp. 197–220

West, S. (1995) *Your Rights 1995–96: A Guide to Money Benefits for Older People.* London: Age Concern England

West, S. (1997) *Your Rights 1996–97. A Guide to Money Benefits for Older People.* London: Age Concern England

Willcocks, D., Peace, S. and Kellaher, L. (1987) *Private Lives in Public Places.* London: Tavistock

Williams, T. and Field, J. (1993) *Pension Choices: A Survey of Pension Choices in Comparison with other Pension Options.* Research Report No. 22. London: HMSO Department of Social Security

Wood, S. (1995) *Residential Care for Older People: the Concept of Choice.* Warwick: University of Warwick & Social Care Association

Woods, R. T. (1989) *Alzheimer's Disease: Coping with a Living Death.* London: Souvenir Press

Worsley, J. (1992) *Good Care Management: a Guide to Setting up and Managing a Residential Home.* London: Age Concern England

Wright, F. (1986) *Left to Care Alone*. Aldershot: Gower

Wright, F. (1992) *Fee Shortfalls in Residential and Nursing Homes: the Impact on the Voluntary Sector*. London: Age Concern Institute of Gerontology/ Association of Charity Officers

Wright, F. (1993) 'Handling residents' monies in residential and nursing homes: an exploratory study', Report to Age Concern England

Wright, F. (1994) *Paying the Price*. Oxford: Anchor Publications

Wright, F. (1995) *Opening the Doors: A Study of Multi-purpose Residential Care Homes*. London: HMSO

Zarit, S. and Whitlatch, C. (1992) 'Institutional placement: phases of transition', *The Gerontologist*, Vol. 32, No. 5, pp. 665–72